Fine WoodWorking on Planes and Chisels

Fine WoodWorking *on* Planes and Chisels

29 articles selected by the editors of *Fine Woodworking* magazine

The Taunton Press

Cover photo by Richard Newman

First printing: January 1985
International Standard Book Number: 0-918804-28-0
Library of Congress Catalog Card Number: 84-052099
Printed in the United States of America

A FINE WOODWORKING Book

FINE WOODWORKING® is a trademark of The Taunton Press, Inc.,
registered in the U.S. Patent and Trademark Office.

The Taunton Press, Inc.
Box 355
Newtown, Connecticut 06470

Contents

Introduction

Woodworking is basically a reductive craft. In this way it is quite unlike working with such malleable craft materials as clay, glass or metal. To work in wood is to cut away thin shavings and little chips, until the piece that's wanted emerges from the larger block. The woodworker cannot do much without sharp edge tools.

This book is about planes and chisels, the basic edge tools of the cabinetmaker. With them we can make a piece of wood flat and smooth, precisely to size. We can cut slickly fitting joints, shape edges to a robust or delicate profile, finish surfaces in even the gnarliest woods. Though many regard the woodworker's plane as the most subtle and sensitive of hand tools, good planes are relatively easy to make. In 29 articles reprinted from the first nine years of *Fine Woodworking* magazine, authors who are also craftsmen explain exactly how they choose, make, and use many kinds of planes and chisels, and demystify the knack of sharpening.

John Kelsey, editor

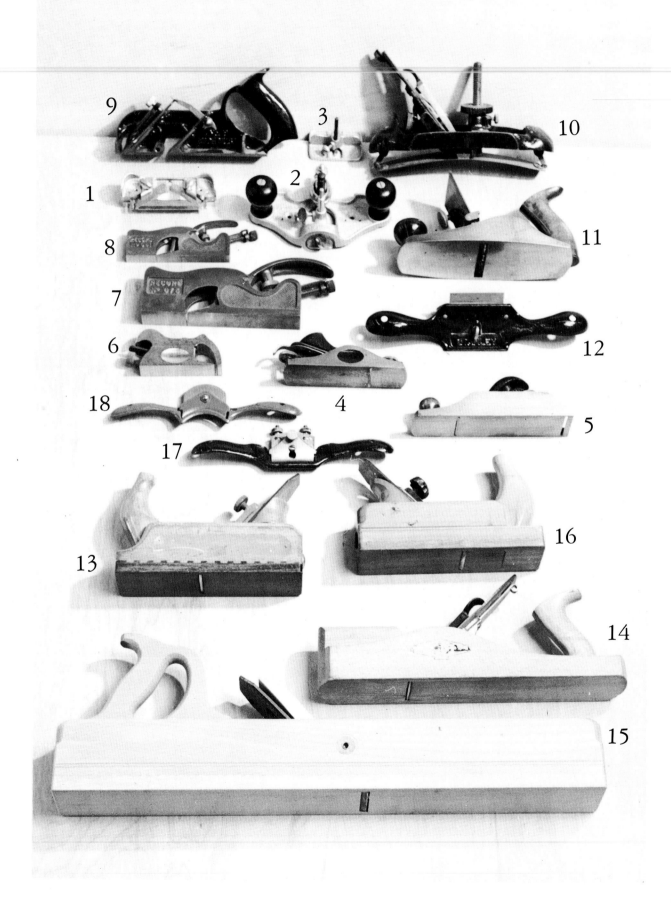

Plane Speaking

One man's guide

by Robert Sutter

Nowadays, when everything in a woodworking shop tends to go buzz, or whirr, or rat-a-tat-tat, or give off some other harsh and less onomatopoeic sound, it is reassuring to hear the ''snick'' of a sharp plane slicing long thin curls off a piece of wood. Reassuring? Yes, for to me the sound and feel of handplaning stock to a smooth surface is a link to the craftsmanship of the past.

I agree it is faster and easier to push a chunk of wood through a machine which automatically makes it smooth, true and dimensioned. But what about the shop which hasn't got 1500 pounds of 18-inch planer squatting there waiting to be run, or a 62 by 9-inch jointer to zip off straight smooth edges? How will you handle the wide board which won't go through either? What to do to smooth a figured table top which the machines would tear to bits? Or fit a door, set in a box-bottom when the box is just the least bit cockeyed, widen a groove a little, or fit a tongue snugly? Easy! Just reach up on the shelf behind your bench and pick off the appropriate hand plane. And which one is that, you ask. Well, I'll tell you what I can about hand planes using the 18 different planes (and spokeshaves) in my own shop as examples. I've taken a family photograph so I can tout them one by one according to breeding and track record.

1. Stanley #79 side rabbet is the only plane which will pare the side of a narrow groove or trim a doorstop in place. It may not be readily available, so buy one when you see it for this plane is most useful.

2 and 3. Stanley #71 and its little cousin, the #271 router, are just the ticket for cleaning up the bottom of lock mortises and hinge butts or truing up the bottom of grooves. The #71 can be used to rout out a groove or a stop-dado if the sides are first cut with a saw. The #271 is great for cleaning up flat backgrounds in carving. Both are designed for use in normal and bullnose positions and are adjustable for depth of cut. (Record, in England, used to make a similar router plane but has discontinued it. The two Stanley planes are still available, but I'd advise haste if you decide you must have them for your shop.)

4. Record and Stanley block planes have irons angled at about one-half that of a bench plane and are set bevel up in an adjustable mouth, thus allowing a smooth cut on end or figured grain. The same features permit taking fine shavings with little or no chance of tearing side grain. Since the block plane fits nicely in the hand, it is useful where stock is held with one hand and worked with the other. Because of its adjustability, the block plane seems to me to be the easiest plane to use when making chamfers.

5. Stanley #130 is the same as (4) but hard to find. It's worth the hunt because a second bullnose-like blade position allows it to get into tight corners otherwise out of bounds to planes.

6. Stanley #90 is a bullnose plane, but also a dandy shoulder rabbet plane since the sides are machined square to the sole. It can also be used as a chisel plane (with bullnose removed to expose the blade completely). I find the plane digs in unless there is a bearing surface ahead of the blade. It is a low-angle, bevel-up, adjustable-throat plane.

7. Record #073 shoulder rabbet plane, weighing in at a tad over four pounds, is the king of planes for accurate work in any situation. A 1-1/4-inch iron set at a low angle bevel-up, an adjustable throat, a micrometer smooth adjustment for depth of cut, beautiful machining and sufficient heft all combine to make a tool which gets a lot of use in my shop. With it I clean up projecting joints, fit tenons, trim edging, true miters, true joined surfaces and rabbets, and on and on.

8. Record #041 shoulder rabbet is just like #073 but only 5/8-inch wide with a fixed nose, and runs a close second for favorite status. Unfortunately, it is no longer available, having been replaced by the #042 (with a 3/4-inch sole but otherwise the same).

9. Stanley #78 rabbet — a workaday plane that somehow survived the Stanley blitzkrieg and is still in the current catalog. It does a creditable but coarser job of cutting and trimming rabbets than (7). Its built-in fence and depth gauge makes for easy, accurate use.

10. My Victor #20 compass plane with adjustable flexible sole is an antique. With it one can plane curved surfaces. A similar plane is now available.

11 and 12. These are both scrapers. The larger one, with a tote and plane-like sole, is the Stanley #112, now extinct. It has a toothing blade for veneering and working curly stock. The other is a Stanley #80 cabinet scraper. Note: wooden toothing planes are still available.

13, 14, 15. These three form the bench plane triumvirate. The foreplane or scrub plane (13) with convex blade will do a fast job of surface cleanup. The jack (14) eliminates most hills and hollows and prepares the surface for final truing with the try plane or jointer (15). I prefer wood planes, but you can get these three in iron with plain or corrugated soles. All work, so it's your choice.

16. This deluxe smoother comes from Ulmia in West Germany. Its lignum vitae sole glides over a surface, and because of an adjustable mouth, the plane can be set to take the thinnest of shavings. It is a finishing tool which leaves an almost polished surface in its wake. Note: wooden planes are now available with screw adjustments under the ''Primus'' name.

17 and 18. These spokeshaves are not planes, strictly speaking, yet they alone will produce a contoured surface or form and smooth work in the round. If you realize that they were used in earlier days to make spokes for wheels, then you'll know what they can do for you.

To be sure, there are a gaggle of other good and useful wood-paring tools I've neglected. But to tell the truth, I was abashed to find as many as I have in and around my bench. I feel that I've covered the most common ground and that perhaps this brief Baedeker to plane-land will help sort out some choices for you. □

Improving Planes
Simple modifications eliminate most common problems

by Robert Foncannon

A finely tuned and smooth-running plane is perhaps the most precise and satisfying tool the woodworker has. I know of no other hand tool that can, with a few easy strokes, remove a shaving only a few thousandths of an inch thick and leave a surface almost as smooth as glass. All the planes in my collection are inexpensive cast iron—they are readily available and are easy to adjust and use.

Unfortunately, most iron planes are not ready for use when purchased. The blades are never adequately sharpened and are rarely set properly into the plane body. The sole of the plane is often not true and usually bears coarse machining marks that impede smooth strokes. The metal adjustment mechanism is potentially very precise, but standard production tolerances allow far too much play. Fortunately, all these faults can be reduced or eliminated. The only power tool necessary for the work is a small bench grinder, with perhaps a cloth buffing wheel in place of one of the stones.

Proper shaping and sharpening of the blade are easy, quick and absolutely essential. Begin by whetting the back surface of the blade on a fine carborundum-type stone, which will cut rapidly without clogging. Hold the blade flat against the stone, bevel up, and whet until the back side is flat and all the machining marks are erased for at least ⅛ in. away from the edge. This step ensures a smooth cutting edge later on. Now, with a try square and a carbide scribe, lightly mark a line slightly to the rear of the cutting edge, on the side just whetted. This line is used during grinding and will ensure a square edge.

Probably more tools are ruined during grinding than at any other time. Following three simple rules will simplify the grinding process and ensure success: Set up the grinder guide system properly for the cut desired, use the correct grinding wheel and dress it properly, and remove metal very slowly to avoid overheating. A blade that has turned blue from overheating will not hold an edge. Grinding the blue away merely masks the damage already done.

In this case, setting up the machine is simple. The tool rest should be positioned so the plane blade intersects the wheel at the desired bevel angle. This allows the blade to be fully supported by the tool rest and restricts each cut to exactly the same angle. I grind all my planes to a 25° angle, though others may vary this a degree or so. A 100-grit wheel is best. It will produce a smoother surface than a coarser wheel, thus requiring much less whetting. Before grinding, be sure to dress the wheel square across its entire surface with a silicon-carbide wheel dressing stick. This not only trues up the wheel to prevent blade bouncing, but also exposes a fresh cutting surface that is less prone to overheating.

Now lightly apply the blade to the wheel. Keep it flat against the rest and in continuous motion to avoid overgrinding and overheating any single area. Dipping the blade often in water helps prevent overheating, though it is not necessary if the grinding proceeds slowly enough. With a little practice and the help of the scribe mark, grinding a straight, square hollow-ground edge is easy. Whetting normally follows next, though I usually complete this step after the other modifications are finished in order to avoid accidently spoiling the edge during handling.

I use a fine-grit India stone for whetting. One side of the stone should be reserved for plane blades and jointer knives exclusively. When this side gets too cupped for proper sharpening, it may be resurfaced by the same method used for surfacing plane soles, described later. The blade should be sharpened on the beveled side, with both edges of the hollow grind touching the stone, until a very small wire edge is formed. Then alternately take a few strokes on each side until the wire falls off. I usually whet plane blades lengthwise down the stone, allowing both edges of the hollow grind to touch the stone, which helps reduce rounding. Whet with a light touch and observe closely, because with proper grinding little whetting is needed. At this point the blade will be roughly as sharp as when new, but not nearly sharp enough for a smooth cut on tough wood.

After whetting, I buff the edge on a stiff cloth wheel

A *properly set tool rest supports the blade and fixes its proper angle to the stone.*

To *buff, pass each edge over the wheel several times with moderate pressure.*

Bevel *behind the chipbreaker edge should just clear the blade.*

mounted on my grinder. The debate over whether to buff or strop is not new. I prefer buffing because it is faster and easier, and the edge it produces will easily shave hair from the back of my hand. I also expect the buffed edge is more durable—less prone to micro-chipping because of its smooth shape. The smoothness also makes a buffed edge less prone to bending.

I load the buffing wheel lightly with tripoli compound and pass each side of the edge over the wheel several times with moderate pressure. The wheel smooths off microscopic ridges rearward of the cutting edge to reduce friction and quickly hones the blade with almost no effort.

Once the blade has been properly ground and whetted, regrinding should not be necessary for quite a long time. Whetting should be done only when buffing is not sufficient to bring the edge back to razor sharpness—generally the edge can be buffed ten to twenty times before it requires whetting, if the blade is not allowed to become too dull each time.

You should regrind when the edge becomes chipped, indicated by a ridge on the piece being planed and by a visible nick in the blade, or when the hollow-ground portion of the edge has been completely flattened by whetting. Regrinding at this point makes the edge easier to whet, because only the leading and trailing portions of the ground edge are in contact with the stone.

The chipbreaker should receive attention next. Its front edge should be exactly perpendicular to the side of the plane blade, and its nose should be sharp—not rounded as most production breakers are. The underside of the breaker edge should be filed or stoned to a slight negative bevel, so when it is assembled to the blade the rear of the bevel clears the blade by about 1/64 in. The breaker edge should be set back from the blade edge about 1/16 in. (less for fine cutting and more for coarse). Proper shape and adjustment of the chipbreaker will help the plane clear itself of debris; improper shape and adjustment will cause problems by promoting clogging of the throat. In some severe cases the top of the breaker edge may need to be filed and polished to make a smooth path for the escaping shaving.

Next, dress the front and rear of the blade opening in the sole so both are parallel and perpendicular to the edge of the plane. This is done by scribing a line on the plane sole perpendicular to the side of the plane and parallel with the opening, and then filing to the scribed line. Use a fine file, remove the metal very slowly, and file away only as much metal as is necessary to square up the opening. Removing more may result in too wide a throat and cause the blade to

gouge. A square opening eases adjustment and simplifies the next step—squaring up the blade support surface.

Many inexpensive planes have blade supports that are not square. This forces the woodworker to set the blade to a compensating angle to get an even cut. Squaring up this surface allows the blade to be set in straight. To make this adjustment, assemble the plane in the normal manner. Use the adjustments and sight along the sole of the plane so that the blade protrudes slightly and is parallel to the plane sole. Now check to see if the blade is parallel with the back of the blade opening and perpendicular with the side of the body. If not, carefully file the support surface under the side of the blade that is farthest forward to produce the proper fit. If the plane has an adjustable frog, see if it can be adjusted to align the blade. The metal on the base of an adjustable frog, or its mating surface on the plane body, may be too rough to permit precise adjustment. File away the roughness on the mating surfaces. The frog should be loosely installed several times during the smoothing process to ensure that the sliding surfaces remain parallel.

After the blade, the blade opening and the blade support have been squared, the width of the blade opening (the throat) should be adjusted, if possible. With the blade in the working position, throat width should be less than 1/16 in. for a block or smoothing plane, and up to 3/16 in. for a jack plane. A narrow opening reduces chatter, especially on end grain, and gouging, but it also diminishes the allowable depth of cut and increases clogging. A block-plane throat can often be adjusted by sliding the front sole plate. On larger planes, the frog is usually movable. When moving the frog, make sure the blade remains parallel to the blade opening. This is important, and should be checked while using the plane. The opening should be as narrow as possible without clogging.

You must be able to set the plane blade to the desired depth of cut. Most new planes have a frustrating amount of play in the mechanism, often a full turn of the knob, despite the theoretical advantages of mechanical coupling over the tedious adjustment of traditional wooden planes. There are three basic types of adjusting mechanisms, and fortunately all of them can be improved with a few simple modifications. The secret is to locate the exact source of the sloppiness. For instance, in the horizontal-screw block plane, play occurs because the fingers engaging the screw are narrower in width than the slot in which they ride. Disassemble the plane and slightly twist the fingers so one is forward of the other. When reassembled, one finger will press on the rear of the slot and one on the front, eliminating the play. The vertical-screw

The edge of the chipbreaker should be set back from the blade edge about 1/16 in.   *This blade, adjusted parallel to the sole (left), is angled because of an out-of-square support surface. To remedy, remove metal from the high side of the support surface (right).*

It's usually necessary to modify the adjustment mechanism to eliminate slop. Offsetting the fingers on the horizontal-screw block plane (left), bending the top finger downward to the nut on the vertical-screw block plane (center), and bending a finger rearward on large horizontal-screw planes (right) help eliminate play. The mechanisms of larger planes are similar to the ones shown here.

To true a plane sole, tape sandpaper to a flat surface and don't rock the plane from side to side. A little water prevents clogging.

The effect of careful polishing on the sole (top) is obvious. Use either crocus cloth or a buffing wheel.

block plane similarly has too large a gap between the fingers of its adjusting lever and the thumb nut. Pinching the fingers together with the thumb nut removed will eliminate most of this play. The horizontal-screw adjusting mechanism commonly found on larger planes has two shortcomings. First, the arms are again too narrow for the width of the slot in the thumb nut, and second, the top ends are too narrow for the opening provided in the chipbreaker. The solution again is simple—just bend one arm forward in relation to the second arm at the top. This bend will tighten up both areas at the same time. No longer will it require two revolutions of the screw to reverse the direction of blade movement.

The final step in plane optimization is the treatment of the plane sole. Most iron planes are finished on a belt sander. They have sharp corners that can mar work, a rough sole that is hard to slide along wood, and the sole may even be convex at the mouth, or dubbed off at the front and back. These problems are easy to solve.

First, smoothly round the corners of the leading and trailing edges of the sole with a fine file. Some woodworkers prefer to square off the rear of the sole (normally slightly rounded) before rounding the edges. The side edges should also be rounded, but to a lesser degree. The sole of the plane should then be ground flat and polished.

The best way to true the sole is to tape a sheet of 240-grit silicon-carbide paper to a flat surface (table saw or jointer table) and slide the plane in a circular motion over the paper.

Be certain the plane does not rock from side to side. Turning the plane end-for-end and lapping in the opposite direction prevents a too-regular pattern and helps produce consistent results. When truing large planes, it may be necessary to tape several sheets together to get enough surface. Use a small amount of water to lubricate the process and keep the paper from clogging. This operation will quickly show up high spots, usually around the edges, and should be continued until all high spots are leveled and there is an even pattern across the entire sole. Next, use wet 400-grit paper and stroke the plane linearly to remove scratches left by the coarser paper. Using 600-grit paper as a third step reduces polishing time later on. A cloth-backed abrasive, such as commercial aluminum oxide, can be used dry in place of the 240-grit silicon-carbide paper. It is more expensive per sheet, but it is more durable and will hold up to the pressure of lapping.

After truing, the sole should be polished. Crocus cloth can be used in a circular motion to polish the sole to a mirror finish, but this is time-consuming. It is faster to polish the sole on a buffing wheel loaded with black emery compound followed by tripoli and rouge. This will quickly bring the sole to a mirror finish. A coat of paste wax will finish the process and leave the sole smooth and slick. □

Robert Foncannon, of East Lansing, Mich., is an electrical engineer who spends his spare time rebuilding used woodworking equipment.

Souping Up the Block Plane

It's a matter of geometry, plus perception

by Richard S. Newman

This tuned block plane easily smooths a curly maple strip that showed severe tearout after a pass over the jointer.

Imagine trying to hand-plane a strip of curly maple sawn to one-sixteenth inch thick, or a one millimeter ebony veneer. This is daily work for luthier Robert Meadow, who creates exquisite lutes of exotic and highly figured woods. As every musician knows, some instruments must be forced to make sound, while others sing at the slightest touch. So it is with tools. Meadow's planes consistently take shavings you can see through, the full width of the iron and the full length of the board.

This is not just extraordinary skill at work. Meadow has spent years investigating how edge tools work. His desire to share his experiences has led to the formation of a school providing intensive instruction in hand-tool work, and to frequent workshops across the country where he impresses audiences with his ability to plane the nastiest wood. I visited Meadow at his school and workshop in Saugerties, N.Y., and discovered that he has evolved to almost exclusive use of Japanese edge tools, both in his own work and at his school. He is convinced that these tools are the ultimate solution to cutting wood. I wasn't ready to take that plunge, so I asked him to share his earlier work with metal planes. In this article I'll describe how Meadow would turn an ordinary block plane into a fine finishing tool.

To begin with, Meadow claims that for fine work, hand tools are a practical, even superior, alternative to machines and abrasives. Planes remove wood a lot faster—and cheaper—than sandpaper. The surface is clearer, feels better and is far more beautiful than an abraded one. Of this last I have no doubt, as Meadow later planed half of a 1/16-in. curly cherry veneered tabletop for me on a visit to my own shop, in order to relax after a trying workshop. His surface was so much better than the adjacent sanded surface that I was in-

spired to tune up my own planes in order to complete the job. You can test this by applying a coat of oil to a wood surface sanded as smooth as you can get it. The oil will soak into the minute scratches that were left by sanding, leaving a dull surface that will require many coats of oil to improve. Apply oil to a planed surface and even the first coat will gleam.

Meadow says, "Tools, hand and power, are really only kits as they come from the manufacturer." Getting the most from a tool means not only mastering its use, but understanding how its design works and tuning it, or even reworking it, to do its job. A razor-sharp edge won't take a good shaving if the plane's bed is warped, nor will a perfectly lapped sole help a plane if its blade is sharpened at an inefficient angle. All the components must be balanced.

In order to soup up a plane, we must try to understand what happens between the cutting edge and the wood. Textbooks contain complex formulas on the subject, but Meadow bypasses the mathematics and goes directly to the results, talking in terms that craftspeople can understand.

A balance of forces—There is a complex balance of forces and resistances when you plane wood. *Back pressure* is the sum of all forces acting to keep the cutter out of the work. Some back pressure is due to the resistance of the wood to being cut, and some comes from friction generated by the plane's sole. Too much back pressure requires excessive effort. *Cutting pressure* is the force the blade exerts as it cuts the wood. A sharp blade working at the correct angle exerts only a small amount of cutting pressure, just enough to sever the wood fibers right at the cutting edge. If the pressure at the edge overcomes the fiber strength of the wood very far ahead

Fig. 1: Plane geometry

A secondary microbevel deliberately honed onto the face or back of the plane iron will increase its cutting angle (**A**) or reduce its clearance angle (**B**). This can help you in dealing with ornery woods, reduce deflection and chatter, and prolong the life of the edge.

Honing the iron with a soft strop or a buffing wheel is liable to add an unwanted, rounded microbevel. On the face of the iron (**C**), a rounded bevel will increase the cutting angle. On the back of the iron (**D**), it may so reduce the clearance angle that the iron can't cut at all. Bearing down too hard while sharpening is liable to reduce the sharpening angle and leave a fragile edge (**E**).

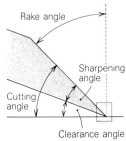

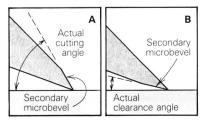

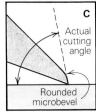

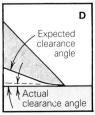

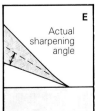

Fig. 2: Bench plane vs. block plane

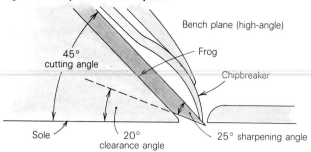

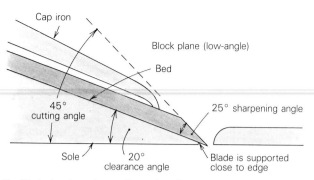

A high-angle plane and a low-angle plane can both have the same clearance angle, the same sharpening angle and the same cutting angle. But the low-angle plane suffers less from deflection and chatter because its blade is better supported at the cutting edge.

The block plane's cutting angle can be adjusted by honing a secondary microbevel on the face of its iron, and this change does not affect its clearance angle. But a secondary bevel on the bench plane's iron reduces only its clearance angle, without affecting the cutting angle.

of the blade, hardwoods will tear out, and softwoods will compress and crush. *Leverage* refers to the tendency of the cutting pressure to bend or deflect the blade at the cutting edge. Leverage varies according to the bed angle, the cutting force and how well the plane body supports the blade.

Edge geometry—The geometry of the cutting edge—its cutting angle, sharpening angle and clearance angle—are familiar concepts, but they can be deceptive (figure 1, page 7). Slight changes in the angles right at the cutting edge, made by microbeveling or stropping, can yield actual working angles that are very different from those built into the plane. These angles can easily be varied and balanced to suit particular jobs.

The *cutting angle* affects the amount of cutting pressure and the way it is applied to the wood fibers. Softwoods generally require a lower cutting angle than hardwoods, otherwise the wood can crush ahead of the blade. On highly figured hardwoods, a low angle introduces a riving action that causes tearing out. Western planes have a variety of cutting angles ranging from bench planes at 40° to special scraping planes at 115° or more. For a block plane, the cutting angle is actually determined by the *sharpening angle,* as shown in the comparison between the bench plane and the block plane in figure 2. By varying the bevel angle or by adding a microbevel not much wider than the shaving is thick, you can, in effect, change the design of the plane. On a bench plane, the sharpening angle is a compromise. The lower it is, the sharper the edge (but thinner, more fragile and more subject to deflection); the higher the angle, the sturdier the edge, but increasing the sharpening angle simultaneously reduces the *clearance angle.*

Clearance reduces back pressure. The cutting edge must press downward, thus compressing the wood as it works, but the wood springs back immediately after the cut. The clearance angle makes space for this expansion. Harder woods require less clearance, while softer, more compressible woods require more, but all woods require some. Insufficient clearance causes friction that heats the cutter, dulling it quickly. A plane iron loses clearance as it dulls. This tends to hold the blade out of the cut, so that the plane skids without cutting.

Why choose a block plane?—Metal planes can be divided into two basic types: bench planes (high bed angle, bevel down) and block planes (low bed angle, bevel up). These planes can look very different yet have essentially the same clearance angle and cutting angle. The ubiquitous Stanley and

Record bench planes are a good example of high-angle design. The cutting angle is set at 45° by the frog, and the clearance angle varies according to the sharpening angle. These planes suffer badly from leverage problems and blade deflection, causing chatter and torn wood, because the blade is not supported close to its edge. This weakness is compensated for by the chipbreaker, a misnomer, as its function is more to pre-stress the cutting edge than to break the chip.

In a block plane, clearance is built into the design by the plane's bed angle. This angle is usually either 20° (Stanley No. 9½) or 12° (Stanley No. 60 or 65). Because the block plane's iron is mounted bevel up, clearance can be modified only by adding a microbevel to the back of the blade, or by stropping. The bed supports the blade right up to the edge, effectively eliminating leverage problems. The cutting angle is variable, determined by the sharpening angle. Meadow says that most woodworkers will find a low-angle block plane to be the best bet for tuning up as a fine finishing plane.

Tuning a plane—For this article, we modified an old No. 9½ block plane. Start by making sure that the back of the blade is perfectly flat, by truing it on a series of stones, on plate glass with carborundum powder, or on diamond-coated steel plates (EZE-Lap-Diamond Sharpening Products, Box 2229, Westminster, Calif. 92683). Then check the mating of the blade to the bed, especially right at the throat. Coat the back of the iron with machinists' layout dye or artists' oil paint (phthalo blue works well) and position it on the bed. When you remove the iron, blue dye on the bed will mark high spots that need to be filed down. If there is any space at all between the iron and the bed, it will fill with dust as you work, deflect the edge, and cause uneven shavings. Remove the burr left by hand-filing, then square up the front edge of the bed by filing a narrow land, just wide enough to see.

Now flatten the bottom of the plane, with the blade tightened in place so the plane body will be stressed as in use. Lap the sole flat or have it ground flat by a machine shop (see article on page 57). This cures the common problem of a store-bought plane that bears down most at its ends, leaving the plane body unsupported at the cutting edge and inviting chatter. The plane actually needs to bear only at its throat and at both ends of its sole. Meadow speeds the flattening process by using a ball mill in a Dremel tool to hollow out parts of the sole, much as the Japanese relieve the soles of their wooden planes. This looks terrible, but it reduces friction and back pressure without affecting the tool's stability.

Its sole relieved with a ball mill to cut friction, the plane bears only at its ends and its throat, and leaves a smooth surface.

Now the iron must be properly sharpened. Meadow shapes his bevels flat, not hollow-ground, in order to limit deflection. He shapes the primary bevel to about 25° and then hones the secondary microbevel to whatever angle works best. Steels vary. For any blade, if the sharpening angle is too small, the blade will tend to chip. If the angle is too large, the blade will get dull a little more quickly. It's a lot easier to hone a blade sharp again than it is to reshape a chipped edge. So each time he hones a particular blade, Meadow gradually makes the sharpening angle smaller until the blade starts to chip, then he retreats. The ordinary alloy-steel iron in the No. 9½ plane is prone to chipping even when sharpened at 25°, so we thickened it up by putting a few degrees of microbevel onto its flat back side. This simultaneously reduced the plane's clearance angle, which is generally not a good idea. But the 20° clearance angle built into the No. 9½ is several degrees more than necessary for planing hardwoods anyway.

The edge of the plane iron should not really be straight but slightly convex, so that a full-width shaving will feather out to nothing at its edges. Meadow makes this curve by bearing down more at a corner as he sharpens. The amount of curvature is greatest on a roughing plane and least on a fine plane: it should approximate the thickness of the shaving.

Meadow cautions that too much pressure when sharpening distorts the metal at the cutting edge. When the metal springs back, the blade has an actual sharpening angle smaller than anticipated. This results in too thin an edge which, although sharp, will quickly break down.

Meadow does not use a leather strop because its surface is too soft. It rounds over the edge, changing the plane's geometry. Instead he makes a hard strop from fine-textured wood—cherry, pearwood, poplar or basswood—planed even and smooth, not sanded. He then rubs a little wet mud from his waterstones onto the wood. When the abrasive mud dries, the strop is ready. Meadow recommends the same procedure for honing carving gouges. Take a pass with the tool on a piece of scrap, and you've made a wooden slip-strop that matches its curvature. After stropping, Meadow washes the blade and his hands in clean water to remove abrasive particles, and then wipes the blade dry and laps it on the palm of his hand.

Adjusting the throat opening is the last step before making a shaving. The throat should be narrow enough to compress the wood ahead of the blade, but when the blade is sharp, the throat opening isn't critical—tearout will be prevented mostly by the geometry of the cutting angle. As the blade dulls, narrowing the throat will eliminate some tearout, but friction

and heat will increase the rate at which the blade dulls, and may even draw the steel's temper. Again, a balance is necessary.

Now the plane should work perfectly. If he encounters problems with a plane, Meadow doesn't automatically blame the cutting edge, but rather looks to see if the planing action is imbalanced. The tightness of the cap iron, for instance, affects both the plane body and the blade. When your plane is set up perfectly, you will find that you can vary the thickness of the shaving just by tightening or loosening the cap iron.

Meadow quotes the Japanese saying, "A master is the person who sharpens least and has the sharpest tools." The real enemies of a sharp edge are friction and impact. Dragging a plane backwards across the work, between strokes for instance, dulls the blade, as does too narrow a throat or insufficient clearance. The most dulling part of the cut is the impact of forcing the edge into the wood in the first place. As long as the edge is firmly in the cut, and doesn't chatter, it dulls relatively slowly. A well-tuned plane helps keep edges sharp. Meadow adds that oiling the cutting edge reduces friction. A thin film wiped on with the fingers is enough, but it must stick to the blade and not be wiped off. Meadow uses camellia oil, but olive oil also works well.

The next step in tuning up a plane, Meadow says, would be to replace the standard blade with one made of laminated steel. Japanese plane irons are laminated, but practically impossible to fit into a metal-bodied plane. Another possibility is to use an old iron from an antique wooden-bodied plane. These heavy, tapered cutters are made of mild steel with a forge-welded edge of high-carbon steel. The qualities of the carbon steel and the forging process create an iron that is capable of taking and holding a much keener edge than the alloy steel used in modern irons, which compromise cutting qualities for ease of manufacture. It would probably be easiest to adapt a laminated iron to a bench plane rather than to a block plane; some ingenuity would be required, but in the long run it might be well worth the trouble.

In woodworking, as in any discipline, the best work can be done only when our tools inspire us. Whether they are antique or modern, Western or Japanese, the challenge is to use them to their fullest potential. But in the end, says Meadow, a craftsperson's most valuable tools are his or her own perception and understanding. □

Richard Newman is a furnituremaker in Rochester, N.Y. Robert Meadow's school is The Luthierie, 2449 West Saugerties Rd., Saugerties, N.Y. 12477.

Useful Second Lives
Saving and using old planes

by Harry Moos

Just a few more strokes on the oilstone and the blade is finished. I look at its edge against the light and there is no reflection. I reassemble the plane and run it over a long piece of pine. The first shaving is too thick. Another adjustment, and then a paper-thin shaving curls away down the length of the board. I make another half-dozen passes before I blow away the bits of wood clinging to the blade, wipe away the fingerprints with an oily cloth, and place the plane on the shelf that I have reserved for it. This once dirty, dull and rusted piece of iron from a flea market has become a polished, sharpened beauty, ready to take its place among my other old tools. At times like this, I honestly don't know if I love the tools because they enable me to work wood, or if I work with wood because it gives me a good reason to collect these fine old tools.

I always return to this cabinet filled with hand tools: the line of planes with flaming rosewood handles, the brass-bound levels and squares, the boxwood rules, the rows of chisels and gouges. I take them from their places, test their blades against my thumb, and replace them. I find no such pleasure in turning the big table saw on and off, or in stroking the plastic surface of an electric drill. These power tools were bought new and are serviced regularly; they serve me well in the hours we spend together. But when I am not working, or perhaps while I am pondering some problem with the wood, I take a spokeshave and a scrap of wood and make a stack of shavings. It is very satisfying.

Here is an auction bill for the coming weekend that lists various carpentry tools, including planes. I have 22 working metal-bodied planes; why do I want another? There might be a Stanley No. 95, or even the elusive little No. 2. It's more likely that I'll find a common smoothing or jack plane, but even so, it may have a corrugated sole or a rosewood handle. There is always excitement in such an auction. What will I find? A few months ago it was a perfect Stanley No. 45 with all the blades still in the original box. Nothing really rare, but nice. And last year I found that beautiful old Stanley No. 72 chamfer plane.

If it is old, I can usually count on the metal being good, the balance right and the handles comfortable. Its modern counterpart will be painted to hide its rough casting, and the handle will be plastic—or, if wood, rounded only enough to delay the inevitable blisters for a few minutes longer. The trademark will not be cast into the body, but will be a decal, as though the manufacturer hopes you will forget who made it as soon as the decal peels off.

Here is an old 2-in. gouge with P.S. & W. Co. stamped on the blade. The handle was missing when I found it in a pile of rusted iron. Someone had beaten the socket with a hammer before discarding it. I could have bought a new one for the time I spent re-shaping the socket and turning a new handle with a leather cap. But when I notice the thickness of the metal and how well it takes an edge, I am glad that I was there to rescue it.

That explains the duplicates here. I can't bear to throw away any good tool that still has life in it. So many people will never know any tools but the bargain from the discount store. Surely someone will want my rescued tools someday, perhaps my grandchildren. So I go to auctions and look for tools at flea markets. I drive around the block in heavy traffic because I see an old plane hanging in the window of a second-hand shop. All in the hope of adding something else to my cabinet of wonders.

Back in the car, I test the metal with fine steel wool to see how bad the rust is and to check the stamped markings. The rust is loose, with very little pitting. And here is the patent date. Yes, it is what I thought.

In the shop, I take the plane apart, sometimes after soaking it in a lubricant if the screws are stubborn. I carefully clean the metal with steel wool, or perhaps a buffing wheel if it will not damage the piece. I may clean threads on a fine wire wheel and blue the steel where it was so originally. If the japanned finish is damaged, I apply new enamel and put the plane body in the oven to dry. Then I clean the wooden parts, fill chips and holes, and apply a finish coat of satin varnish, or maybe just wax.

These may not be the proper steps for someone interested in preparing a tool for resale on the antique market, but I am going to use this tool, not sell it. Occasionally I have to weld some part, or replace missing parts from my box of odds and ends. Some tools have been waiting for years for this piece of brass or that kind of bolt. Finally I grind and hone the blades.

I am especially fond of planes, shaves and chisels because they make shavings. I love a good old brass backsaw, too, but it makes only dust. I used to wonder about an old neighbor who sat for hours whittling, stopping only to spit tobacco and sharpen his knife on a little stone—not making anything, just cutting big sticks into little slivers. Now I think I know what he was doing. Because when I smooth a board with a plane, I too am fascinated by the shavings that curl away in delicate spirals. □

The Stanley #55
Understanding an ingenious workhorse

by Gregory Schipa

The Stanley #55 Universal Combination Plane, because of its apparent complexity, is often relegated to the collector's shelf. But you can put it back to work.

Most people, when they first set eyes upon a Stanley #55 Universal Combination Plane, are sure they've discovered the ultimate contraption, though one undoubtedly too crazy to work. That's what I first thought, yet many years later the #55 has grown to be a part of me. As the Stanley Tool Company modestly described it in their 1897 catalog:

> Combining as it does all the so-called 'Fancy' Planes, its scope of work is practically unlimited, making the Stanley #55 literally 'A planing mill within itself.'

I have my reservations about that sweeping claim, but there is no doubt that for the cabinetmaker, house joiner or restorationist, the #55 is a most useful and even addictive tool. With a little patience, you can set it up to do the job of any one of a hundred specialty planes, and it will duplicate period moldings you simply cannot find in the lumberyards, nor even mill with a spindle shaper.

History—Although the #55 seems to have landed from space, it is actually the product of a gradual, rational evolution. In the 19th century, single-purpose wooden planes, basically the same design as had been used in ancient Egypt and Rome, had multiplied until a cabinetmaker or housewright might have needed a hundred of them to fashion all the moldings in style, an expensive and weighty collection to store and transport. These beautiful wooden planes were also un-

stable, liable to check and warp.

The Industrial Revolution provided a metal technology that avoided wood's drawbacks. In 1871, after successfully marketing a series of cast-iron bench planes, Stanley introduced the "Miller Combination Plane" as a replacement for the carpenters' plow—it employed metal screw threads instead of wood, and a sole that "would not warp or swell." Within a few years Stanley came out with the #45, which replaced a boxful of plows, fillisters and beaders. Meanwhile, improvements in machinery resulted in abundant, newly available mill-run moldings, which reduced the need for handwork and hastened the decline of the wooden molding planes. It was only a matter of time until the #55 came along and claimed to be able to take over all molding functions.

My crew and I have four of the contraptions, and they are invaluable for the restoration work we do. It's curious how we came to discover them. I had been using old wooden planes to duplicate moldings, and had even had a few new ones made for me by Norman Vandal (see article on page 30). I'd picked up some old metal planes, too, including a Stanley #45 with interchangeable cutters. I remember musing to myself that the #45 would be able to do just about anything if only it had sole runners that could be adjusted vertically as well as horizontally. And then I discovered the #55, which has exactly this feature. In my own day-to-day work, I'd gone through the same evolution as had a generation of 19th-century housewrights.

The Stanley #55 Universal Combination Plane was developed by Justus A. Traut and Edmund A. Schade, who patented it in 1895. It was first marketed by the Stanley Tool Company in 1897, with 52 cutters (the number gradually climbed to 55), and remained relatively unchanged until it went out of production in 1962. There were 41 optional cutters as well, which are now quite rare. In addition, a craftsman could grind cutters of his own design out of flat tool stock. The catalog listed it as a "molding, match, sash, beading, reeding, fluting, hollow, round, plow, rabbet and filletster, dado, slitting, and chamfer plane." It is 10 in. long and weighs 15¾ lb., including all parts and cutters. The body is nickel-plated, and the fences and handles are rosewood. As much as the following description (quoted from the 1897 Stanley catalog) is a tangle of terminology, to a craftsman who could use this versatility in his daily work it must have been engaging reading:

This plane consists of: A Main Stock (A) with transverse sliding arms (H), a Depth Gauge (F) adjusted by a screw, and a slitting cutter with stop. A Sliding Section (B) with a vertically adjustable bottom. The auxiliary Center Bottom (C) is to be placed in front of the cutter as an extra support, or stop, when needed. This bottom is adjustable both vertically and laterally. Fences (D) and (E). Fence (D) has a lateral adjustment

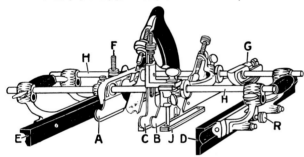

by means of a screw, for extra fine work. The Fences can be used on either side of the plane, and the rosewood guides can be tilted to any desired angle up to 45°, by loosening the screws on the face. Fence (E) can be reversed for center beading wide boards. An adjustable stop (J) to be used in beading the edges of matched boards is inserted on left hand side of sliding section (B). A cam rest (G) aids stability.

The #55 with all its cutters fits in a case the size of a shoebox, and it will produce handmade moldings of considerable depth and classic shape. It was never intended that the combination plane should outperform all individual molding planes, but rather that it should allow the craftsman at the job site to match whatever profile he might need. A #55, trimmed for work, weighs at least 3½ awkward pounds, whereas a small beading or molding plane weighs a balanced and comfortable 10 oz. to 14 oz. Over the course of a day, the difference is significant.

Also, even though the #55 is more straightforward than it at first looks, setting it up takes time. After setting three runners, the blade, two fences, spurs and perhaps the cam rest, you would certainly hesitate before disassembling everything to cut a plain rabbet. You'd grab the nearest rabbet plane—or an electric router—instead.

Despite its complexity, the Stanley #55 becomes easy to understand when you examine its relationship to some of the

planes it replaces. In the drawing on the facing page, for instance, we see three old planes. The first, one of a pair, is a single-purpose plane that makes a groove on the edge of a ⅞-in. thick board (the other plane in the set makes a tongue). The next, a more versatile plow plane, has an adjustable depth stop and a fence on adjustable arms. The fillister plane has features that allow it to cut cross-grain rabbets. Both the grooving plane and the plow plane, instead of requiring a broad, flat sole like a bench plane, have a single, thin metal runner that limits the depth of cut on each pass. The main stock of the #55 has a similar runner. With one of its fences attached to the metal arms, the main stock of the #55 would closely resemble a plow plane, as shown at **A**, and, with none of its other parts attached, could be used to plow a narrow groove. A wider iron, however, such as cutter no. 15 in the small drawing below, would be difficult to use with a single runner, because if the plane tilted at all, the cutter would dig in. The #55 therefore has a second runner that can support the other side of the iron, as shown at **B** on the facing page. These two runners suffice for most of the #55's cutters. By designing this sliding-section runner to be vertically adjustable, Stanley made the plane capable of reproducing wide flutes (cutter no. 55) and thumbnails (no. 64), as shown at **C**. An auxiliary half-runner is used to support the middle of the wider cutters when necessary.

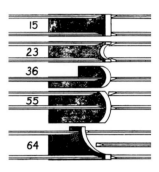

How it works—Setting the heights and locations of the runners is the key to setting up the plane. Two pairs of arms

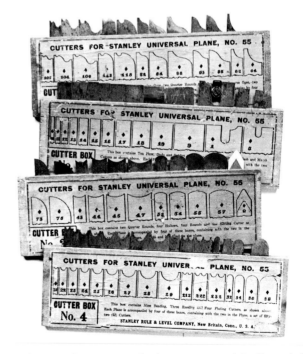

Stanley's 52 (later 55) standard cutters were originally packed in flat wooden boxes. There were 41 additional cutters available, wider and narrower versions of the basic shapes.

Fig. 1: Evolution of the #55

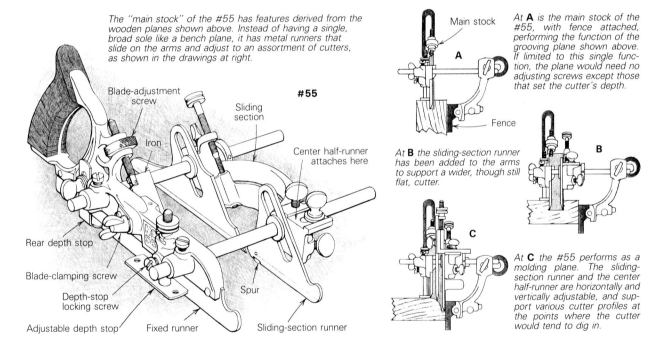

Wedge

Metal runner

Iron

Metal runner is "sole"

Depth stop

Fence

Grooving plane

Grooving plane has only one function, hence no adjustments except for the wedge that locks the iron at the correct depth. The metal runner acts as the sole, preventing the iron from digging in. Fence and depth stop are built-in.

Adjustable depth stop

Iron

Adjustable fence

Plow plane

Plow plane, with adjustable fence and depth stop, makes grooves on the face of a board. Some plows have assorted blades of different widths; with others you plow grooves side by side if you need one wider than the iron.

Depth stop

Spur

Boxwood insert

Iron

Adjustable fence

Fillister plane

Fillister plane's fence and depth stop are adjustable. A sharp spur severs the wood fibers ahead of the iron, allowing the plane to work cross-grain. For efficiency, the iron is wider than the cut; the fence adjusts beneath it.

The "main stock" of the #55 has features derived from the wooden planes shown above. Instead of having a single, broad sole like a bench plane, it has metal runners that slide on the arms and adjust to an assortment of cutters, as shown in the drawings at right.

#55

Blade-adjustment screw

Iron

Sliding section

Center half-runner attaches here

Rear depth stop

Blade-clamping screw

Depth-stop locking screw

Adjustable depth stop

Fixed runner

Spur

Sliding-section runner

Main stock

A

Fence

At **A** is the main stock of the #55, with fence attached, performing the function of the grooving plane shown above. If limited to this single function, the plane would need no adjusting screws except those that set the cutter's depth.

At **B** the sliding-section runner has been added to the arms to support a wider, though still flat, cutter.

B

C

At **C** the #55 performs as a molding plane. The sliding-section runner and the center half-runner are horizontally and vertically adjustable, and support various cutter profiles at the points where the cutter would tend to dig in.

come with the #55: one set is 4½ in. long, the other is 8¼ in. long. To adjust the plane for different cutters, you simply slide the runner sections you need onto the arms, then clamp them in place by tightening the wing nuts. Runners, when you are using them at the outside edges of a cutter, should be set as close inside each edge as possible, so that they can bear against the sides of the groove being cut. To set the proper exposure of the cutter, I find it simplest to set all the runners exactly flush with the cutting edge, then to lower the cutter. This is easily done by turning a single, knurled nut—it tracks the iron up and down with almost no play.

The cutters: The 96 factory-made cutters, shown in the photo at the bottom of the facing page, are used one at a time in the #55. When a combination molding must be made, a series of shapes can be planed next to each other

until the profile is complete. You usually plane the part of the profile farthest from the fence first, working progressively toward the edge of the stock on which the fence rides. Also, you must plane each shape on all your sticks before you

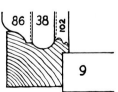

change the cutter for the next part of the profile. It is tricky to maintain consistency, and a slip in any one of the operations means that you've ruined your molding. You need to plan for a lot of wasted sticks. I find that the moldings created this way are the least effective use of the #55 plane. Stanley liked to think that there were virtually unlimited options and combinations, and technically there are. Most combinations of cutters on a single piece, however, take considerable sawing and rabbeting in combination with the actual molding cuts. This is extremely time-consuming. Combined moldings usually come out a bit inconsistent as well. Instead, it is more practical to make a series of separate moldings, then combine them, such as by nailing on a cove-and-bead below a reverse ogee to form a nice cornice molding.

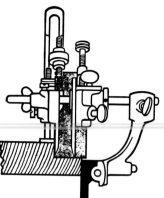

The fences: The #55's fences can be adjusted up and down—by means of alternative holes for the arms—as well as in and out. They also tilt to 45° for making chamfers. There are two major fences that come with the #55. The larger one has adjustment screws that help in setting the fence vertically parallel to the side of the cutter. Keeping the fence flat against the work is the best way to keep the plane perpendicular. If the fence is not parallel to the side of the cutter, the plane will run either into or away from the work, binding and cutting poorly. Stanley suggests using both fences whenever possible (one on each edge of the stock), but I find that this causes the plane to bind, and mostly I just use the smaller one.

When you use the plane, keep pressure toward the work, so the fence won't ride off (especially on coves and thumbnail moldings). Also, to keep the plane running straight, push the #55 with your right hand only—use your left hand to keep inward pressure on the fence.

Depth stops: The main depth stop adjusts with a single knurled nut. It works like the depth stop on the fillister plane shown in the drawing on page 13, eventually contacting the top surface of the work and preventing the plane from cutting too deeply. There is another depth stop, located on the main stock behind the blade, which should be used whenever it can make contact. When you use the front depth stop alone, the plane tends to tip back. In addition, some of the cutters accept a little, built-in depth stop that can be adjusted with a screwdriver (note cutter no. 1 in photo on page 12).

The spurs: The main-stock runner and the sliding-section runner both have adjustable spurs located just in front of the blade. As in the fillister plane, these sever the fibers ahead of the iron for a cleaner cut, and they must be kept sharp.

The slitting cutter: A knife-blade-like cutter can be set into a holder located behind the usual blade location. It is used to split strips off the edge of boards—similar to a Japanese splitting gauge—and works faster and more neatly than a saw on thin stock.

Primary functions—Perhaps the function for which the #55 is best suited (or at least most easily applied) is beading, the creation of a small half-round with a groove (called a quirk) on the edge of a board, or occasionally in the middle. A bead was most often applied to embellish the joint (and to disguise wood movement) between two matched boards, or as the inside edge of window and door casings. If the cutter, depth gauge and fence are set properly, the bead will be perfectly shaped. A flat-topped bead means the depth is set too shallow; a flat-sided bead means the fence is too close to the blade. If there is a flat on the outside of the bead, the fence is too far from the cutter (you have created an astragal). The most common mistake in beading is letting the fence ride away from the work, which results in an enlarged quirk, and a shrinking bead.

Rabbets and grooves are simple with the #55. It is always easiest when rabbeting to use a cutter wider than the rabbet.

The smaller fence can be adjusted so it bears on the edge of the stock below the blade, as shown at left. The plow function is accomplished very handily as well, although the narrower cutters are best.

Of the "fancier" moldings, the #55 cuts some well, but it makes others only with difficulty. The Grecian ogees (cutters no. 102-106) seem to work most easily, because the plane has less tendency to ride off the piece. On these and all fancy moldings, however, you must take care not to roll the plane out, or the moldings will be uneven and impossible to join on the same work without carving. Profiles that drop off away from the work tend to encourage this riding-off. Coves, Roman ogees and reverse ogees fall into this category, and the simple "thumbnail" or ovolo cut on the edge of a stile is the most difficult (the cutter is referred to as a quarter hollow). These cuts all call for a very shallow blade setting, and strong pressure toward the work. On many, Stanley recommends that you leave some stock uncut on the outside edge, as shown at left, to be trimmed off later. This traps the bottom runner and prevents it from sliding off the work.

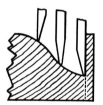

Availability—Stanley's "miracle" tool is out of production. The combination planes that are on the market (the best two I've seen are the Record #405 Multi-plane and Stanley's #13-050 Combination) do not have the vertically adjustable fence and thus lose most of the functions that made the #55 so versatile. With the resurgent interest in hand-tool work, the popularity of the #55 is again growing. Unfortunately, these planes are usually found at the antique tool dealer's, where demand from the tool collectors, the nemesis of the joiner and cabinetmaker, has driven up the price. The planes seem to be harder to find each year, but the major dealers can usually come through with one for about $200 to $350 (1983), a price comparable to a new combination plane.

The number of cutters will vary according to the year that the plane was manufactured, but check to see that most of them are there and in good condition. Check the rest of the parts against a complete list (available from Stanley), and examine the castings for small hairline stress cracks, especially on the depth-gauge housing. Also check that the runners are not bent, but perfectly parallel. A hint: never put a #55 where it can fall from the bench—the results are disastrous. When you get your new/old plane home, keep it well oiled against rust, and spend some time sharpening and honing your cutters—they have to be perfectly sharp. ☐

Gregory Schipa, of Waitsfield, Vt., is president of Weather Hill Restoration Co., which takes apart period houses and refurbishes them. The Stanley Tool Co. will supply instruction booklets to owners of the #55 (write R. West, Manager, Product Research Standards, Stanley Tool Co., 600 Myrtle St., New Britain, Conn. 06050). A 1980 reprint, The Complete Woodworker, *edited by Bernard Jones (Ten Speed Press, PO Box 7123, Berkeley, Calif. 94707), has 16 pages on the fine points of the #55.*

Putting an old #55 to work

by T.D. Culver

If you decide to buy a Stanley #55, first examine the plane body and all the parts for broken castings, bent runners and chipped cutters. A plane with bent or broken castings has been dropped and will be cranky. A "bargain" on a #55 may be no bargain. I would not buy one sight unseen.

If the plane is okay, check the cutters. Ideally, the bevels should still have the grind marks from the factory. If any of them have been badly honed, their profiles will be wrong. Count the cutters. My #55 came with 52 of the 55 regular cutters, including two sash cutters, and none of the 41 special cutters. I have yet to find a molding I cannot duplicate.

There are two positions for setting up the stock to be molded: on edge in the vise or flat on the bench. It is difficult to hold a piece narrower than about 2 in., so glue it temporarily to a waste piece. After molding the shape, saw it free.

If you are starting with a wide board and making narrow moldings, plane one edge, flip the board (paying attention to grain direction), and plane the other edge. Rip these moldings off, joint the edges and begin again. You can turn out a surprising amount of molding in a fairly short time.

The position of the stock determines how the fences will be set on the #55. When the stock is on edge, it is extremely useful to set up both fences, because then there is no worry of tilting the plane and spoiling the molding. Set the left-hand fence, place the #55 on the stock, and tighten the wing nuts

as you squeeze the fences together hard. When you begin planing, there will be quite a bit of resistance, but it soon eases.

When you're planing work flat on the bench, the dogs and vise may not hold it against the considerable side pressure you need to exert. Or the board may not be wide enough to be clamped in the dogs and still overhang the benchtop. A few finish nails through the work and into the bench will hold and will not foul the fence arms. You can support the ends of long stock on sawhorses.

Usually only one fence can be set when the work is laid flat, which allows the #55 to tip and ruin the molding. After five years of struggling, I finally acquired a cam rest and it is worth every penny I paid. Contra the instruction manual, I set it opposite the fence on the front arm. By adjusting the screw so that the cam rotates stiffly around the fence arm, I can set the bottom of the cam even with the edge of the cutter. Now the #55 rides on two points instead of one. As the cut progresses, the cam pivots and continues to hold up its end of the plane. Be sure to twist the cam back to its original position when you start to plane another stick.

The cutter should protrude beyond the runners at the sides, just as it must at the bottom. Otherwise the runners will foul the molding. The depth of cut should be set very light for molding and slightly heavier for plowing. The runner on the sliding section may creep, causing the cutter to dig in, unless the thimble check-nuts are tightened. These are round, knurled nuts located on the out-

side of the sliding section through which the fence arms pass. Finger-tight is usually enough, though there are holes for a tommy bar. If the plane throat jams with shavings, you are taking too heavy a cut. Check that the sliding section hasn't crept up, or reset the cutter higher in the plane body.

You will find vernier calipers a great help in setting up the #55. Once the cutter is fixed, set the depth stop with the calipers, measuring to the cutter edge, not the runner. Then set the fence, measuring at both the front and the back, so that it is parallel to the runner. Be sure to square the bearing face of the fence to the fence arms.

It is especially important to plane through the work in one continuous stroke. Choppy strokes will choke the plane and damage the molding. Clear a space in front of the bench and walk through each stroke with firm pressure against the fence. Shavings will curl out like excelsior and wind around your wrist. Clean out the throat when you're walking back for the next stroke, so the plane won't jam.

Clear wood is best, although very small, tight knots can be molded, with luck, in an easily worked wood such as walnut. Straight grain is helpful but not essential on many shapes.

The #55 is surprisingly effective in rabbeting and plowing plywood. Some split-out can be expected, but a heavy knife cut on the layout lines will minimize this. In desperate straits, costly hardwood plywood can be jointed, plowed and splined just like solid wood. The #55's no. 12 cutter makes a nice groove for ¼-in. fir-plywood splines.

The major problem with any antique plane is finding parts, although some parts for the Record No. 405 Multiplane do fit the #55. Cutters for the Multi-plane fit both the #45 and #55, but the selection is not as vast as the original Stanley cutters. The fence arms are the easiest to replace—pieces of ⅜-in. mild steel rod work just fine.

I've had my #55 for six years, and every year it seems to work better and better. It is a complex tool, and it takes some time to learn well. That time will be amply rewarded one day, when you stand ankle deep in shavings and hold up to the light a crisp molding fresh from the plane. □

T.D. Culver is a carpenter and cabinetmaker living in Cleveland, Ohio.

The #55 in full array, geared up to plane a quirked bead on a pine board.

Gregory Schipa

The Legendary Norris Plane
A hard-to-find tool that's worth the search

by Edward C. Smith

The London firm of Thomas Norris and Sons made exceptionally fine woodworking planes from about 1860 to 1940. Their products, especially the smooth plane which is the subject of this article, are arguably the finest planes ever manufactured. Although expensive, they are prized by cabinetmakers and tool collectors. For the worker who handplanes regularly, and who appreciates fine tools, the Norrises are worth knowing about.

I have owned a Norris smooth plane for about three years, and have used it on timbers ranging from docile cherry to hard, contrary ebony, cocobolo and bird's-eye maple. It invariably performs better than other metal or wooden planes I've used, producing a fine finish even against the grain and adjusting easily for the finest shavings.

In concept the Norris is simple. It's a metal box—mild steel plates dovetailed together, or a single-piece iron or bronze casting—stuffed with rosewood, beech or occasionally ebony. The plane's virtues accrue from this construction. Any Norris is about 1½ times heavier than the equivalent Stanley, so it hugs the work with an inertial force that makes planing easier. The cutter is twice as thick (3/16 in.) as that in a comparable Stanley-type plane and is firmly bedded on a large wooden frog, a combination that virtually eliminates chatter. The adjuster is precise, moving the iron horizontally and vertically with little of the play that plagues other planes.

The Norris has a further virtue: it's beautiful, particularly the early, rosewood-filled versions. Most models are graceful and fit the hand well, and the contrasting colors of steel, bronze and rosewood attract the eye. Since few of us would regularly work a Norris to the limits of its capability, the ultimate justification for ownership must be somewhat subjective, the feeling that comes from owning the best. One more reason for owning a Norris is as an investment. Demand from workmen and collectors has pushed Norris prices steadily upward, and this trend shows no sign of change.

If you buy a Norris, there are important caveats to note. The Norris was produced in four product lines, each with a range of models. Only some of these are worth considering. The costliest Norris planes were made of bronze with steel soles and rosewood or ebony infill. They are heavier than other Norris planes and striking in appearance. But the slight advantage of their greater weight is counterbalanced by their extreme rarity and high price, about double that of the comparable steel or iron versions.

The dovetailed steel models filled with rosewood are much more common. These are the "classic" Norris planes most prized by workmen, and the ones generally thought of when the marque is mentioned. These were made with either curved or straight sides, with open or closed handles, and in a curved-sided version without a handle.

Next in price were some annealed cast-iron planes, cheaper because they required less skilled handwork and preferred by

The Norris adjuster mechanism consists of a steel eyelet with an attached rod threaded into the adjuster shaft. The eyelet engages the cap-iron screw to raise or lower the iron. To align the cutting edge, the shaft pivots on a cylindrical knuckle.

some because they are heavier than the joined steel planes. Except for the model A15, which I own and consider quite attractive, I find most of these planes a bit homely.

There is a subgroup of cast-iron planes worth noting. During its later decades, Norris made iron planes in a curved-sided model similar in appearance to the steel planes and filled with stained beechwood. Though not as attractive as the classic-period planes, they retain all the practical virtues of the Norris, including—except as noted below—the adjuster. These planes are relatively common and often available in good condition at half or two-thirds the price of a rosewood model. Unfortunately, some of these later planes have a cheapened version of the adjuster. The better adjuster consists of a threaded rod within a threaded sleeve, permitting precise turning. The cheaper model has no sleeve, resulting in an adjuster with more play. There's generally no difference in price so avoid those with the poorer adjuster.

Least expensive in the Norris line were cast-iron planes with model numbers 49 to 61. These are of much lower quality than the general line, and were meant to compete with Stanley-type planes, which were becoming very popular by the turn of the century. They are Norris in name only, like a downsized Cadillac, and may be of interest only to collectors.

My choice of planes today would be the curved-sided models A2 (open handle), A5 (closed handle) and A4 (no handle), which are all of the classic dovetailed steel type; the cast-iron A15; and, only if available at a much lower price, the beech-filled iron model.

With model numbers in mind, check the following points when examining a plane for purchase, or when instructing a dealer regarding a mail-order purchase.

The plane body: This is crucial. I know of no way to repair a cracked casting or battered and bent steel plates. Such damage has likely forced the sole out of truth. Rust, if superficial,

Where to look for a Norris

Besides smoothers, Norris made panel and jointer planes; shoulder planes; miter, rabbet and bullnose rabbet planes; and chariot and thumb planes. For a survey that includes two Norris catalog reprints, write Ken Roberts Publishing Inc., Box 151, Fitzwilliam, N.H. 03447. Below is a list of dealers who may have Norris planes for sale, or who will accept a standing order.

The Mechanick's Workbench
PO Box 544, Front St.
Marion, Mass. 02738.
Iron Horse Antiques, RD 2
Poultney, Vt. 05764.
Tom Witte, Box 35
Mattawan, Mich. 49071.
Roy Arnold, 77 High St., Needham Market, Suffolk IP6 8AN, England.
Philip Walker, Beck Barn
The Causeway, Needham Market Suffolk IP6 8BD, England.

Sources for Norris cutters:
Henley Plane Company, 13 New Rd., Reading, Berkshire, England, will make irons to fit pre-war Norrises in the 2⅛-in. to 2⅜-in. sizes.
London Auction House occasionally has second-hand irons: Tyrone Roberts, Watton Rd., Swaffham, Norfolk, England.

The Norris plane is considered by many to be the Rolls-Royce of hand edge-tools. This model A15 smoother has a one-piece cast-iron body and rosewood infill and handle, a construction that makes it 1½ times heavier than an equivalent Stanley-type plane.

can be removed with steel wool or fine emery. If the metal is pitted, the plane's market value may be lowered, as will its utility if the sole is scarred. Offer a lower price for a plane with pitting on the sides. The sole can be resurfaced by a machine shop or by laborious hand-lapping.

Wood parts: The condition of the wood parts is more important in fixing price than in determining utility. In fact, some look-alike Norris competitors sold just the plane body, leaving the customer to make his own infill and handle. The workman willing to repair or replace damaged or missing wood parts may be able to acquire a perfectly serviceable plane well below the usual price.

The adjuster: This mechanism is simple, quite heavily constructed and not likely to be damaged. And a damaged or missing adjuster can be reproduced by any competent machinist. Many adjusters are fastened to the plane frog with special screws requiring a custom-made screwdriver. Further, it appears that the screws were driven home before the lever cap was installed, so their removal requires a right-angle driver even if the screw heads are common.

The cutter: The back of the cutter, opposite the bevel, must be free of all but the mildest rust. It should be perfectly flat and highly polished. Pitting will require grinding and lapping, or machine-shop services. Remember, the Norris has no provision for frog adjustment; making the cutter thinner by surface-grinding may open the mouth more than you want. The frog can be shimmed, but this isn't good practice because the iron's firm bedding is at the heart of the Norris' performance.

Plane irons, of course, wear away as they are sharpened, so most Norrises are likely to have partly used-up irons. When new, a typical Norris cutter would have had about 2¼ in. of usable blade below the cap-iron screw cutout. I would try to get a cutter with at least 1 in. of usable blade. When I needed replacement irons a couple of years ago, I discovered that

they are scarce and expensive. I purchased mine from Roy Arnold for £15 (about $22 in 1983) each plus shipping from England. Except for collectors, it is not important that the cutter be stamped with the Norris name, but it should be the right width and it must be a "gauged" or "parallel" iron. This means that it is the same thickness throughout its length rather than tapered like irons in most wooden planes. In a pinch, a tapered iron can serve, but as the iron wears through sharpening, the mouth of the plane will widen. The cap iron should be original, since the adjuster works by receiving the cap-iron screw. Check that the cap iron mates properly with the iron—no light should show between it and the cutter when they are tightly fitted.

Against this background, the question is: where to find a Norris and how much to pay? Norris planes were imported to America, but they aren't likely to be found at a garage sale, an antiques shop, or even an old-tool shop. American buyers should contact dealers who specialize in British tools. I know of only two, both mail-order, who have had more than one or two Norris planes over the past three years (see box). You may need to place a standing order with a dealer for a specific model. Specify the condition of the plane you want, including what sort of damage you consider acceptable.

Prices for antique tools are fairly volatile, but you can make an educated guess after perusing a recent auction catalog. I would expect to pay about $300 to $350 (1983) for a rosewood-filled smoother in one of the desirable models, and about $200 to $225 for a beech-filled model. Though expensive compared with other hand planes, Norrises are a bargain measured against the labor it costs to buy one: about a week's pay, both in the 1920s and today. □

Edward C. Smith lives in Marshfield, Vt., where he makes furniture and tools.

Japanese Planes
The preparation and use of *kanna*

by Ted Chase

Woodworkers, both amateur and professional, have been hearing lately about Japanese tools. Ads mention "superior edge qualities," pulling instead of pushing, and assorted other exotic advantages. Interested people who have purchased a Japanese tool may have brought it to the shop, used it for a while and gone back to work with their original tools. Others have found that the tools they bought "didn't work" at all. As with all fine tools, knowing how to care for and prepare them is essential for premium performance.

A brief history — Probably the most striking thing about traditional Japanese woodworking is that much of it is done in a sitting position. The earliest of Japanese tools, the *chona*, or adze, was used long before the introduction of the ripsaw (late 14th century) to rough-surface lumber that had been split with wedge and/or chisel. The adze handle was wood and the blade socket was of primitive and thin metal. A person's full, standing force behind this tool would break the socket—thus the seated position. Nor was this unusual to the lifestyle. Japanese homes have long been designed for multiple-purpose living with minimal furniture; sitting on the floor has been the typical posture for work and for eating. Woodworking was similar. Because few woodworkers had large, permanent shops, a great number of master carpenters, carvers and apprentices would be gathered for a commission by an emperor, feudal lord or military leader. These artisans would set up shop at the construction site, so putting the work on the ground eliminated the need for a workbench. Since less power was applied to the work, it required no mechanical clamps or vises. Because the adze was used across the grain rather than along the length of the piece, the stroke was shorter and a worker could keep one hand free to hold or position the piece. Both feet were available as clamps and weights. Even today, Japanese craftsmen prefer to work sitting down. And where workbenches are used, they're much lower than Western benches, and without vises. The worker planes against a bench stop. Because the bench is low, he can place a foot or leg up on it to hold down the work.

It wasn't until the late 1300s that Japanese blacksmithing and iron manufacturing improved significantly. Along with the refinement of military weapons and ceremonial swords came the introduction of the ripsaw. Lumber cut with these saws could be surfaced more smoothly with a new tool introduced from China via Korea. Its blade, stronger than the *chona*, was set in a block of wood that was moved over the length of the piece to yield a smooth, flat surface. These planes, as used in China and Korea, were designed to be pushed, not pulled. The early imports had a dowel or piece of wood used as a handle, extending through either side. However, these handles soon disappeared, and the craftsman pulled the plane over the work from a seated position.

There have been numerous explanations for the reluctance of the Japanese to adopt the push stroke. Earlier tools and the lifestyle had established deep precedents. Pull-type crosscut saws were used as early as 800 A.D. Given the state of the blacksmith's art at this time, thin blades did not have the stiffness to be pushed through the wood. Perhaps the pull stroke in carpentry goes back to the earliest farming methods, characterized by pulling the hoe rather than plowing through the soil. Consider too that the most common and cherished building materials were straight-grained cedar and cypress; saws and other tools do cut these better on the pull stroke.

Japanese planes have changed little over the centuries. Unlike Western planes, which began in wood and matured to metal (and now are back to wood), the block of solid wood, usually oak, is still the basic modern Japanese plane. The only major refinement came in the late 1800s with the introduction of the subblade, or chipbreaker, positioned a fraction back from the tip of the primary blade.

A *kanna* is simpler than the standard metal block plane. It has no handle, no adjusting mechanism, no screws and levers—just a solid block of wood with two blades wedged in behind a pin that runs the width of the body. The design has been the same for 400 years. Its components are the *kanna no ha*, the plane iron, and the *dai*, the body.

The *ura* face — Most Japanese cutting blades, whether used in planes, chisels, gouges or spokeshaves, are different from Western blades. The standard Western blade is a solid piece of high-carbon steel. The steel of a Japanese blade is a laminated composition of high-carbon and low-carbon steel. The angled or beveled side, *omote,* is never double-beveled. And the other side, *ura* (the flat side of the Western tool), has a hollow ground. The laminated composition and hollow-ground shape offer a number of advantages. The actual cutting edge is the high-carbon steel and the rest of the blade is softer, more pliable steel, which can absorb shock when planing a board with knots or irregular grain patterns; the blade has less tendency to skip or chatter as the plane hits an irregular point. Another advantage is that the hollow-ground section of the *ura* side does not require regular attention. Because there is less surface area, it offers less resistance as it is guided over a board or grinding stone, so keeping this side flat and sharp is easy.

The first procedure in the preparation and care of any Japanese tool with this kind of blade is to obtain a completely flat surface on the *ura* side. Instead of a grinding stone, a *kanaban*, or "iron board," is used in conjunction with a series of grinding powders beginning with *kongosha*, a coarse material from sandstone. The other two powders are residual

Ted Chase, who now makes furniture in Concord, Calif., spent a year in Japan studying with master craftsman Kennosuke Hayakawa.

grinding material that comes from the medium and fine grinding stones. A pinch of *kongosha* is dropped on the iron board with a bit of water and the flat surface of the blade is ground back and forth, yielding a streaked surface. When the streaks are uniform over the face, wash the board and continue with a pinch of the second grinding powder, residue from the medium stone, and a bit of water. This yields a finer, but still streaked, surface. When the streaks are uniform, wash the board again and continue with a pinch of the third grinding powder, from the finishing stone, and some more water. The final step is to put only a drop of water on the board and work the blade face over the board until it is completely dry. Continue to work the blade on the dry surface until there is a completely unstreaked mirror finish on the *ura* face. This is the "basic face" because it is prepared first, after which it remains relatively untended.

The *omote* face — The next step is to sharpen the beveled side of the blade, the *omote* face, on the medium stone. The *omote* face is a bit more difficult to prepare than the basic face, because only the angled part of the blade is held against the stone so it is easy for the blade to twist or roll. The medium stone is also used with water, not oil, and kept clean when not in use by being submerged in water, usually standing on one end. When sharpening, add enough water to provide an easy, but not resistance-free, movement across the stone. As you sharpen, water and stone material will ac-

cumulate at both ends of the stone. Save this as the second powder for the iron-board treatment of the *ura* face. As you sharpen the bevel, a burr will develop on the cutting edge, felt from the *ura* side. When it spans the entire cutting edge, change stones and work with the finishing stone. Grind only the *omote* face on the medium stone, never the *ura* side.

Begin on the finishing stone by working the *omote* face in the same manner as on the medium stone.* Then turn the blade over and work the *ura* face over the stone as done on the iron board to begin to remove the burr. Return to the *omote* face and work, then back to the *ura*. The ratio of working the *omote* to working the *ura* is about 10 strokes to 2. Continue until the burr is gone from the *ura* and a mirror surface appears on the *omote*.

Obviously you should keep your iron board and stones completely flat. Sharpening thin blades that do not cover the entire surface of the board or stones can change their shapes. To keep them flat, sharpen on different areas of the board or stone, covering its full length. Check the surface regularly and, as needed, rub together two wet stone faces, of different

---

*The medium stone is usually synthetic. The finishing stone comes in both synthetic and natural stones. I use the King deluxe 1000 (available from Woodline/The Japan Woodworker, 1731 Clement Ave., Alameda, Calif. 94501). I have both synthetic ($15 to $25) and natural ($50 to $5,000) finishing stones and find the synthetic adequate for the average worker. However, as one's techniques become more refined, the natural stone is, subtly, much better.

Omote, or beveled side of a kanna *blade, left, reveals laminated composition: high-carbon steel at the edge; softer, shock-absorbing low-carbon steel for the rest of this side, including the back of the bevel, which appears lightest in this photo. The* ura, *or basic face, right, is hollow-ground.*

Japanese *kanna*

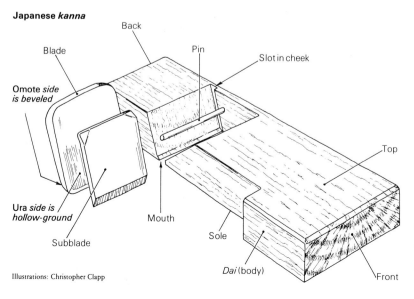

- Blade
- Back
- Pin
- Slot in cheek
- Omote *side is beveled*
- Ura *side is hollow-ground*
- Subblade
- Mouth
- Sole
- *Dai* (body)
- Top
- Front

Illustrations: Christopher Clapp

A kanaban, *or iron board, sharpens the* ura. *A series of grinding powders pictured at top— kongosha, right (a sandstone grit), and second and third grinding-stone residues, center and left— are mixed with water on the* kanaban *and the blade ground back and forth over it to bring up a mirror finish. Bottom, because of the low-carbon steel in the blade laminate, the hollow ground on the* ura *can be pushed out by tapping the bevel on the* omote *with the pointed edge of a hammer while the blade rests on the corner of a hard metal surface. This is done when, after repeated sharpenings, the edge has been ground back into the* ura *hollow.*

or of the same grit. This can also be done with two iron boards, with water in between.

Refinishing the *ura* — It would appear that when the *omote* has been sharpened and resharpened down to the hollow itself, the cutting surface has run out. When the front edge can no longer be worked or sharpened, the hollow-ground surface of the *ura* must be pushed out, providing more surface area for the basic face. Because of its low-carbon-steel composition, you can tap the *omote* face with the pointed edge of a hammer to push the *ura* face out.

Hold the *ura* face tightly against an anvil or the edge of a heavy metal work surface. With the blade at a 45° angle to the edge of the anvil and using the pointed edge of a hammer, gently tap the *omote* face along a line across the whole face. The line, actually a series of indentations, must be made two-thirds of the way down from the tip of the blade. Steady, firm taps are necessary, spaced right next to each other in an even line. Later, with proficiency, it will be possible to tap the line halfway down from the tip. This takes less time but more skill. An improperly placed tap can seriously damage the blade. Use gentle, yet firm and evenly placed, taps. Too much force can crack the blade.

This completed, return the blade to the iron board and, using the second powder, begin to rework the basic face. If the front edge does not yet yield enough high-carbon steel, return to the anvil and begin again. This process cannot be hurried, and you may have to repeat it a number of times.

A good blade made of high-quality metal can last a lifetime if it is treated with care and respect. Many old Japanese craftsmen are proud of their *chibi*, or shortened blades, reshaped and sharpened through many years of work.

Usually, the first 15 mm of a new blade does not produce the finest-quality edge and cut, not because the steel is different from the rest of the blade, but rather because through a process of sharpening, finishing, shaping and refinishing, the blade is tamed, custom-fitted to the craftsman. And in some ways, the blade tames the worker as well: The particular composition of each blade is different, so through use and care, a worker will come to understand what is expected of him. Over a period of many years a craftsman will be able to determine which planes to use for rough work and which for finish work, which for soft woods and which for hard.

Using a finely tuned blade becomes an experience in feeling, or "tasting" with one's hands. The taste is different for each person, depending on the style of work, and comes only with experience. But, by watching a good craftsman at work, one can see the plane cutting smoothly over any angle of grain. Then, if the blade tastes like it is not cutting (not passing smoothly over the wood), a sensitive and patient worker will stop, return to the medium stone and resharpen the blade. This takes place many times during the course of a day whenever the blade is not cutting the way it should feel.

The *dai* — I have been told of legendary master carpenters who could sharpen their plane blades so keenly and prepare the *dai* (the plane body) so finely that if they placed the *kanna* on one end of a board and tilted the board, the plane would cut by itself as it slid down the board. Carpenters' mythology, perhaps, but it sets a standard of excellence that these craftsmen are constantly trying to achieve.

Preparation of the *dai* is essential to proper tool care and functioning. Because all Japanese planes are made of solid wood and affected by changes in temperature and humidity, *dai* preparation becomes an ongoing technique for the life of the plane. Improper *dai* preparation probably causes the most problems for those Western woodworkers who buy a Japanese plane and find it useless from the start or after the first change in the weather.

Usually the blade of a new *kanna* does not fit down completely into the mouth and extend out enough to cut. This is sometimes because the seasoning process continues after the *kanna* is manufactured. The first procedure is to correct the groove in the *dai* for the blade to fit snugly, yet deeply enough to cut. In *kanna* with both a blade and a subblade, to allow adequate room to work on the groove, remove the pin that holds the subblade against the main blade. Place the *dai* on its left edge and grasp the pin tightly with pliers. Tap the pliers firmly with a hammer. When the pin protrudes from the hole in the side of the *dai*, pull it out with the pliers.

Now using a short-bristle brush, paint ink on three sides of the main blade. Do not ink the *ura* face or the cutting bevel itself. Chinese calligraphy ink is best. Before the ink dries, place the *omote* face against the angled groove of the *dai* and push in by hand. Gently tap the top end of the blade down further, using a metal hammer with a convex face or a wooden mallet. The tapping should become increasingly firm until the blade fits in the groove. Listen, and when the sound is "solid" (a higher-pitched tap) the blade is snug. To remove the blade, tap the end of the *dai* (behind the blade) firmly with the hammer until the sound indicates the blade is loose. Tap the upper corner-edge of the end of the *dai* on either side of the midpoint, first one side then the other, back and forth. Be sure to tap the corner edge squarely so as not to chip the *dai*. By placing the thumb of the hand holding the *dai* against the blade, you can exert pressure outward with the taps of the hammer, which will also prevent the blade from shooting out of the *dai*, and onto the floor or your foot.

With the blade removed, you can chisel away the ink impressions left on the tight parts of the groove and refit the blade to sit deeper in the *dai*. Chiseling should remove only a thin amount of wood, almost like a powder, and the process of inking and refitting the blades is repeated many times. Chisel only on the wide face that touches the beveled side of the blade and along the sides where the blade fits into the groove; do not chisel the top of these side grooves.

When refitting the blade, don't force it any deeper than it can go with gentle to moderate tapping. Again, listen to the taps. When you begin to sight the blade along the sole of the *dai* just protruding from the mouth, the process is complete. It will take time, especially when the plane is new. After that it won't be necessary to refit unless the temperature or humidity changes significantly or the seasoning process is still extremely active. Then minor inking can be done.

The process sounds complicated and time-consuming, but it is necessary and, with practice, easy. It might happen that too much of the groove has been chiseled. In this case, glue a piece of paper on the wide part of the groove that supports the *omote* side of the blade.

The sole — Sometimes planes are used on their sides, planing, for example, on a shooting board. The Japanese *kanna* is tipped on its right side for this. The sole and right side of the plane therefore must be square. Planing the side might be

Paint the lower face and the two edges of the blade with ink, left, and while the ink is still wet, tap the blade in to register the high points in the groove. When the blade is tapped out, ink remains on the areas to be pared down, above.

necessary. Be careful when chiseling the groove to fit the blade. After many years you may weaken the right side with excessive chiseling, so favor it.

The next step in preparing the *kanna* for use is to make the sole completely flat. The best method for doing this uses a special plane called a *dainaoshi*, whose single blade, set at 90° in the *dai*, scrapes fine, powder-like shavings from the sole of the *kanna*. It is possible to use a wide chisel in the same way. (In fact it is necessary to correct the sole of the *dainaoshi* itself in this way.)

By holding a straightedge across the sole of the *dai* in front of a light and tilting it slightly, you can watch for light to shine through underneath and illuminate the high and low spots across the surface of the sole. Hold the straightedge in many different positions: along the width, length and diagonal. Move it slowly and mark the high spots with a pencil.

Now take the *dainaoshi* (or a chisel) and begin removing the pencil marks, and with them a thin shaving of the sole. Be sure to plane evenly so as not to create extremely low or twisting spots. It is sometimes wise to plane across the *dai* from one side and then turn the *dai* around so planing can go across from the opposite side. This will ensure even planing. Always plane across the *dai,* not lengthwise. You can, however, turn the *dainaoshi* at different angles to the sole of the other *kanna* to smooth the planing action. After removing the pencil marks, again check for flatness with the straightedge and mark new pencil lines for the next shaving. Repeat until you've rendered the *dai* completely flat.

Some books, both English and Japanese, suggest using coarse abrasive paper to sand down the sole of the *dai* to flatness. However, this method is not advisable. The grit from the paper can lodge itself in the sole of the *kanna* and can mar the surface of the lumber being finished. It can also transfer grit into the lumber and then chip the blade as the *kanna* makes its next pass. Further, any other method of treating the sole after sandpaper has been used risks damaging the tool used for the second refinishing.

Depending upon the climatic conditions of the shop and the seasoning qualities of the *dai*, secondary *dai* refinishing with the *dainaoshi* will be necessary at various times. Again, the feel of the cut is the best way to tell whether you should check the sole for changes in flatness. For the *dainaoshi* and finger planes, a flat sole will suffice for smooth cutting. However, large-body *kanna* require further treatment to

create a "wave" pattern on the sole that facilitates accurate and smooth cutting. Locate four points on the sole of the plane: Point *A* is the front of the *dai*. Point *B* is the part of the sole just in front of the mouth, or opening for the blade. Point *C* is that part of the sole just behind the mouth. And point *D* refers to the opposite end or back.

With the *dainaoshi*, plane the sole between points *A* and *B*, taking care to keep those two points the same height. The area between should be approximately 1/64 in. lower. Now, working back from point *C*, plane *C* just a fraction lower than *B* and continue to plane the sole out toward the back to about 1/32 in. lower than *A* and *B*. By eliminating the surface area between points *A* and *B* you reduce the surface of the *kanna* in contact with the wood. Further, the area between points *C* and *D* is a fraction lower than point *B* or the blade would be lifted off the wood and would not cut, or would cut erratically. The figures given are basic rules of thumb for relative

Not to scale

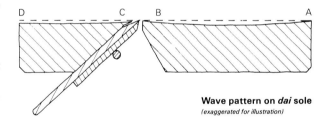

Wave pattern on *dai* sole
(exaggerated for illustration)

Dainaoshi *(planes whose blades are set at 90° to produce a scraping cut for truing plane soles) are used always across, never along, the length of the sole. Larger plane soles are planed not flat but in a wave pattern to reduce friction.*

highs and lows for all points. The best-prepared *kanna* would use fractions of these fractions, and the quality of the cut would be unmatched.

When preparing the sole with *dainaoshi* or chisel be sure to back the blade out of the mouth area, but keep the blade just snug enough in the groove to warrant removal with a hammer, not a hand. This will exert force on the sole behind the mouth so the highs and lows one measures during correction will be the same as when the blade is in the cutting position. Otherwise, the blade might force the area behind the mouth higher than point *B.*

Even after many, many years of seasoning, a *dai* may still need correcting. Again it becomes an experience in feeling to determine when the *dai* is not cutting or moving across the wood efficiently. By examining the sole for shiny spots, you can sometimes detect the high spots without a straightedge. However, this is a preliminary step and should be followed up with the techniques presented here to correct and prepare the *dai* for further use.

Once you've prepared the sole of the *kanna* with a *dainaoshi,* a few minor adjustments must be made for the final finish. A newly purchased plane has a bevel running the length of the *dai* on either side of the sole. After fitting the blade in the *dai,* you'll find these bevels do not reach the mouth. To eliminate unnecessary contact between sole and work surface, increase the size of the two bevels right up to the mouth area. Then chisel a cut at either side of the mouth, angled back toward the end of the *dai* and out onto the beveled sides. This angled cut acts as an escapement for fine shavings that would otherwise become clogged in the mouth. Finally, on the upper edge of the mouth, or the edge closest to the back of the *dai,* chisel a thin 45° bevel across the entire edge. This bevel can reflect light and silhouette the blade as one sights it down the length of the *dai,* facilitating easy and proper gauging of the blade depth.

These procedures may sound complicated. One might ask, "Why not the marvels of modern metal planes?" However, if you are interested in using a Japanese plane and you can complete these steps, you'll be rewarded with an unparalleled

cutting tool that will become easier to operate and to maintain as you work with it. Consider the greater sensitivity of a wooden *kanna* over a metal plane; the pull stroke keeps the work between *kanna* and body. In a short time you'll develop a different sense of control over your work. Another advantage of Japanese planes is that because they are made of solid wood with no moving parts, they can be modified and adapted to fit an infinite variety of shapes and surfaces.

Choosing your *kanna* — The usual manner of making and buying *kanna* in Japan is for a craftsman to purchase one from a master *kanna* maker or from a shop that sells *kanna* made by others. Then he either uses it as is or changes it to suit his needs. The process of making a *kanna* can involve both hand and machine work to a greater or lesser degree, depending on the tool's quality and cost.

I was introduced to a man who makes *kanna* in the Nagoya area of Japan. He and his son run a small tool and hardware shop. They would first cut and square pieces of wood to approximate size using a table saw and a jointer. This wood is then stored anywhere from 2 to 25 years. Much concern and respect are shown for the seasoning process. Better-quality *kanna* are seasoned longest and made by hand. The groove is cut either entirely by hand or with a mortising machine and then finished by hand. The *kanna* master usually buys a variety of blades from different sources, again at varying quality and cost. He builds the *dai* to fit its chosen blade. An expensive *kanna* will have a *dai* seasoned 25 years, and will be made completely by hand, including the blade. It will cost about $250.

Japanese *kanna* can be purchased in a variety of standard sizes. The standard ones are mostly flat-soled. However, it is possible to find tool shops that also sell *kanna* with shaped soles for specialized planing. Finger planes are usually bought in the standard shape and the *dai* recut to fit the job at hand.

Here are some hints on what to look for in a *kanna*. Check the end grain of the *dai;* it should be running horizontally, not vertically as in Western planes. The rays will run vertically and should be well-defined. Check to see that the mouth of the *dai* is not too large and that the escapement angle for the shavings is sharp. There should be no gaps along the groove where the blade fits into the *dai.* To check for this, hold the *kanna* up to a light source and check for light in the groove between blade and *dai.* Test whether the blade fits tightly in the groove. If the *dai* has two blades, it will have a pin to wedge the blades together. Check the positioning of the pin. If the *dai* has been expanding and contracting in the shop, the pin may be pushed through or near the opening of the hole. A tight-fitting blade and evidence of pin movement indicate a better plane; the *dai* has been around for a while, so it is older and therefore more seasoned. Another important thing to check is that the *ura* side of the blade(s) is well shaped and has a well-defined concave face.

The processes involved in preparing and maintaining Japanese *kanna* are rigorous at first. The attention to detail on such seemingly simple tools is, without a doubt, not for everyone. However, for a craftsman who is willing to put mental, as well as physical, effort into preparing and caring for these planes, the rewards can be profound. The craftsman becomes so intimate with his *kanna* that it is, indeed, an extension of his hands, putting him in touch with the process of making, as well as with the end result. □

Kanna *newly purchased, left, and after complete preparation of the sole, right. The large bevels that run the length of the sole decrease the surface area, the notches at the sides of the mouth are for fine-shavings clearance and the chamfer along the back edge of the mouth is for reflecting light to sight proper blade depth.*

Making a Modern Wooden Plane
Nuts and bolts adjuster controls depth

by Karl Dittmer

When I yearned for a quality wooden try plane, I took one look at the price and decided to build one using rock maple. Modern glues are trustworthy, so I elected to build it in four layers, using two ¾-in. pieces for the inner layers and ½-in. pieces for the outer. This made it a simple matter to cut the throat area, usually a chore.

The result was quite successful, except that the old-fashioned wedge system proved a bit coarse, particularly when trying to back off the blade for that final light cut. After some thought, I came up with an acceptable depth adjustment that engages the head of the screw attaching the plane iron to the chipbreaker. I have eliminated free play through careful fitting and now have a precise, uncomplicated adjustment mechanism that is almost as smooth and accurate as the one on a Primus plane I acquired during an extravagant moment. Lateral adjustments are made by forcing the top of the plane iron to one side. Come sharpening time, the homegrown mechanism shines because the iron comes out without any of that Primus-type hassle.

The modernized try plane worked so well, I bought more irons and turned out a few more planes. All are a pleasure to use and construction is simple, thanks to being able to work on the throat area before each is assembled. I make my throats small, then after the sole is finished, file them to fit. Don't despair if you get the throat too big. A thin shim epoxied under the plane iron near the throat opening will cure it.

Most of my planes have the iron at 45°; smoothing planes should be at around 50°. Dimensions were determined by the width of the plane iron and what I felt would be appropriate for my style. If you are not certain just how long to make your plane, make it oversize, then cut it off later. ☐

Karl Dittmer builds furniture in El Reno, Okla.

Photos: Ray Jones

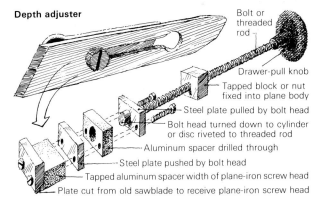

Jack plane, right, with depth adjuster and glued-up body is easy to build; most of the throat area can be sawn before assembly. For stability, grain in adjoining pieces of wood is alternated. The adjustment screw, threaded through a brass block mortised into the plane body, is bound to a sliding carriage that fits the plane-iron screw. After the center laminates are sawn, left, they are positioned on the side pieces using steel pins. The sides are cut with a saw and chisel to taper in toward the mouth. Here Dittmer cuts a mortise to accept the depth-adjustment mechanism.

Depth adjuster

Bolt or threaded rod
Drawer-pull knob
Tapped block or nut fixed into plane body
Steel plate pulled by bolt head
Bolt head turned down to cylinder or disc riveted to threaded rod
Aluminum spacer drilled through
Steel plate pushed by bolt head
Tapped aluminum spacer width of plane-iron screw head
Plate cut from old sawblade to receive plane-iron screw head

Gentleman's plane, disassembled above, is even easier to make than the all-wood-bodied planes. It uses the same adjusting mechanism, but has steel side straps and a pin to hold the wedge and plane iron in. With the toe removed (which reveals its mouth-adjustment capability) and an alternate, shorter set of side straps, it could be used as a bullnose plane.

Some of Dittmer's handmade planes.

Hand Planes

The care and making of a misunderstood tool

by Timothy E. Ellsworth

A plane is one of the most essential tools used by wood-workers and one of the most misunderstood. A simple examination of most modern planes on the hardware store shelf will be proof of this. The bottom will probably be warped and out of true by as much as 1/16th of an inch. There will be rounded edges around the throat or opening, and the chipbreaker will be very coarsely made.

The result is that a significant amount of remedial work is necessary to make the plane function. If the manufacturers don't understand planes or don't care about these potentially precision instruments, then how can the woodworker be expected to understand?

For those woodworkers who have been frustrated by planes or who have given them up completely, the following discussion might help. I am assuming some degree of familiarity with planes to the reader, but recommend *Planecraft*, published by C.P.J. Hampton, Ltd., Sheffield, England, for fundamental reading, as well as the booklet, *Planes*, published by Stanley Tools.

Let me begin by describing the qualities of a good metal

A partially disassembled smooth plane. The all-important adjustable frog is between the iron and the plane body. In a block plane, there is no frog; the iron rests on the plane body and a moveable toe plate adjusts the blade opening.

plane, because that is what most people are familiar with. The bottom must be flat, really flat: no warp, no dips or hollows. There must be some provision for varying the opening, either by means of an adjustable throat (used in block planes) or a moveable frog (used in bench planes). The bearing surface for the iron must be flat and free of burrs and irregularities. There must be a cap iron or chipbreaker, except in the case of block planes. Adjusting knobs and lateral adjusting levers are normal on all but the cheapest planes. The steel in the iron must be of high quality, but this is rarely a problem.

Most of the planes that you will find in hardware stores will have uneven bottoms. There was a time when plane bottoms were precision surface ground, but cost cutting by manufacturers has, for the most part, eliminated this expensive process. The common practice now is to surface plane bottoms on abrasive belts. The result is a less-than-true bottom.

Truing and tuning your metal plane

The surface you are planing can be no truer than the bottom of your plane. You have two options in truing up the bottom. One would be to take the plane to a machine shop and have it surface ground. This might cost about $20 to $30. The second option is to lap it yourself. This process is very simple and requires a perfectly flat piece of 1/8 or 1/4-inch glass at least 12 by 12 inches and some fine abrasive powder such as silicon carbide which can be found at many auto-body shops or art suppliers. Get both 400 grit and 600 grit.

About one-half teaspoon of the 400-grit powder is sprinkled on the glass with about one teaspoon of water. The plane bottom is placed on the glass and a figure eight grinding motion is used, keeping even pressure on the plane all the while. Use the entire surface of the glass to keep the wear even. In a short while the abrasive will become worn out and it will be necessary to rinse the plane and the glass in water and start again.

After repeating the process several times, inspect the bottom of the plane. The dips and hollows will show up as shiny spots not yet touched by the lapping. Continue lapping until they are eliminated and the entire plane bottom is uniformly grey. At the same time the plane bottom is being ground, so is the glass. So try to grind the glass uniformly to avoid making it hollow.

If the glass was flat to begin with and the lapping uniform, your plane should be perfectly flat and true. At this point it is a good idea to lap once or twice more with 600 grit to bring

Once you've made your first plane, there's no limit to the different ones you can make. Here's a sample of those made by the author.

up a fine finish. Although it is not necessary, you can polish the bottom with jeweler's tripoli polishing compound. After this step, scrub off the tripoli residue with soap and water. I like to use a touch of paraffin to lubricate the bottom as I plane, but this may cause problems later if you plan to use a water stain on the planed surface.

Sometimes the surface of the frog on which the iron rests will be very rough. In this situation lapping can be used to make it flat and help prevent the iron from chattering while planing hard woods.

While I am talking about plane bottoms, I might mention the other maintenance which you can do from time to time. Quite often the plane bottom will get nicked, especially on the edges. File or lap off any of the burrs resulting from these nicks. They will show up as lines, even grooves, in planed surfaces.

With the plane bottom now perfect, you will need to set the opening, a most important step usually overlooked. With the iron sharpened, honed and set in the plane, adjust the iron to the maximum depth of cut you expect to make. The

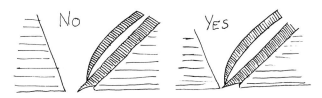

resulting opening in front of the iron should be barely enough to let the shavings through easily. If necessary, remove the iron, loosen the frog screws and adjust the frog. Check the opening again. This opening will be especially critical for very fine cutting in hard woods, curly grain, and for final finish work. Let me repeat that the opening should be as small as possible, but yet let the shavings through easily.

The next concern is the chipbreaker or cap iron. It must be

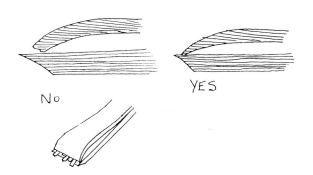

properly seated on the plane iron. First make sure that the flat side of the iron is just that: flat. There is a tendency when honing the flat side to round it over slightly at the edges. This will cause trouble. Once the iron is flat the chipbreaker should seat on it perfectly when tightened. If you hold it up to the light there should be no light coming through the joint. At the same time the chipbreaker should be sharp right to the point of contact with the iron so that no shavings can get caught or wedged up under it. It will probably be necessary to grind the chipbreaker on your oil stone to make it meet the iron properly.

The chipbreaker should be set back 1/64 to 1/16 inch from the cutting edge of the iron. The closer setting would be used for the very fine shavings on finish work and for hard-to-plane woods. Setting the chipbreaker back 1/32 to 1/16 inch would be for rough work and large shavings. The combined effect of the narrow opening in the plane bottom and the close setting of the chipbreaker causes the shaving to make such a sharp bend that it has no chance of propagating a tear-out ahead of the iron, and leaving a rough surface.

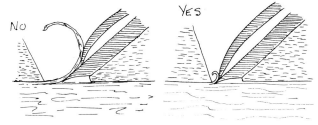

The problems associated with a block plane are not much different than those of bench planes. Because the block plane is used mainly for end grain, the iron is set at a lower angle and is flipped over so that the bevel is up. There is no breaker. The opening is not adjusted by moving the frog, but rather part of the plane bottom at the toe moves backward and forward. The bottom can be ground in the same fashion as the larger planes. One is then concerned only with sharpening the iron, setting the depth, and adjusting the toe plate to close up the opening, as was done for the bench planes.

The uses of planes

To describe the uses of the various planes requires some generalization as there is not much consistency between which planes different craftsmen use for different tasks.

The block plane has two main uses. One is planing end

grain. The other is any planing job requiring one-handed operation. With a low iron angle and the lack of a chipbreaker, the block plane has limited use on long grain because it tends to cause tear-outs.

There is much less consensus on what the specific uses of the various sizes of bench plane should be. There are four common sizes: smooth, jack, fore, and jointer, ranging in size from the smooth (as short as six inches) to the long jointer (24 inches and up). I would venture the following statement: The longer the plane, the less it tends to be affected by local hollows and high points and the easier it is to get a true surface. On the other hand, because of its size and weight, the longer plane tends to be somewhat unwieldy and tiring to use. For larger and longer surfaces it has its advantages. I have seen jointer planes used effectively for everything from six-foot edge joints to three-inch end grain surfaces.

As you might expect, the smaller bench planes such as the smooth plane are much lighter and easier to control, but affected more by the irregularities in the rough wood. Many craftsmen use them, as the name implies, to smooth the marks left by the larger planes. Some might argue that there is really no reason why the larger planes should not leave a smooth surface. In the long run, the individual will find his own preference. The best advice to a potential buyer of a first plane would be to get one of the mid-sized ones, the jack or fore, which are in the 12 to 18-inch range.

A final note on planes and hand tools in general deserves to be made. They are getting harder and harder to find. We have become so dependent on machines that the hand skills are fast disappearing. The manufacturers are responding by dropping many lines. The lines they keep are cheapened since they know that the unskilled public will likely not know the difference. It is sad.

What about wooden planes?

It is fulfilling to make objects of craft or art. To make the tools with which you manufacture the objects is exhilarating. This is the case with wooden planes. They are simply made and can enliven the planing process. As to function, handmade wooden planes can achieve results equal to the finest metal planes—some would say better. They can be made to fit the job: long, short, wide, narrow, curved, flat, or any number of specialized shapes. The plane body can be made to fit your hand and your way of planing. For those who like to work with wood, there is a joy in using a tool also made out of wood.

Are wooden planes better than metal planes? Just about the only factual thing that can be said is that the sole of a wooden plane is less likely to mar the wood being planed. But a wooden plane can't take abuse, so that one's first plane, which does tend to get abused, should probably be of metal. Conversely, a metal plane must be kept tuned to perform right, so that the choice between metal and wood turns out to be mainly subjective.

Materials for making wooden planes

The materials needed to make wooden planes are relatively easy to find. In fact, it is probable that most of what you need can be found in your own shop.

The wood used needs to be a hard, dense wood. We are

aiming for a solid blank to make the plane out of, but in most cases this will have to be glued up from whatever is available to you. Hard maple works quite well, as does beech. In fact, many of the old planes were of beech. Oak is hard enough,

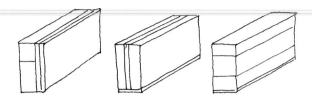

but a little too coarse. Other native woods such as apple, pear, dogwood, iron wood and hickory are excellent, if you can find them. The best yet would be to use some of the extremely dense exotic woods to make a thin bottom to glue onto the main body of the plane. Lignum vitae, cocobola, bubinga, and tulipwood are excellent, but as with all good things, they are hard to find and expensive.

You will also need some 1/2 or 3/4-inch dowels, depending on the size plane to be made, as well as some 1/4-inch dowels.

For the plane iron and chipbreaker, there are a number of options. You can borrow one from your metal bench plane or you can find old ones at flea markets, junk dealers and garage sales. You can also get replacement irons for metal planes at some hardware stores or from the manufacturers. In some cases you might find irons without breakers, in which case it is possible, with a little ingenuity, to make the breaker.

I should note here that you may not have access to the machines mentioned in this project. In this event, planemaking will be a challenge, but still quite possible. You may have to adjust the dimensions and use your ingenuity to compensate for the lack of machines. I have made planes entirely with hand tools, but of course it required a lot of patience, bordering on endurance.

Making the plane blank

Measure the width of the iron to be used and add 1-1/2 inches. That will be the width needed for the blank. Much of the extra material will be lost in subsequent machining operations.

Determine how long a plane you want, add at least four inches (more if possible), and that will give you the length of the blank. In no case should the blank be less than ten inches or it will be awkward and dangerous to machine.

For larger planes the blank should be four to five inches high, and for smaller ones, three to four inches. It is best to err in the direction of making the blank too high. (For purposes of this article, dimensions have been standardized. Needless to say, innumerable variations are possible.)

Dimension the blank. In most cases it will have to be fabricated from two or more pieces of solid wood glued together. Once the glue has cured, the bottom should be run over the power jointer to clean up the bottom and to square it to the sides.

If a special hardwood bottom or sole is to be added, do it now. There is no limit to how thick the bottom can be as long as it is over 1/4 inch. Make it oversize in length and width.

Glue the piece on, let the glue cure, and then plane off the overlapping edges.

With or without the special bottom piece, you should end up with a block that is surfaced and square in all dimensions.

Laying out the blank

Lay the blank on its side and make a mark on the bottom edge where the iron should come through. This should be 1/3 of the distance from the front. Draw a line from this point at 45 degrees toward the rear of the plane. Also mark in a clearance angle. This can be either a straight line at about 60 degrees to the bottom, or a curved line. It should intersect the 45-degree line at the plane bottom.

The center point for the wedge pin must be located, 23/32 inches back of the intersection of the 45-degree line and

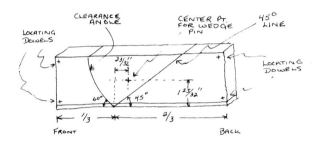

clearance angle, and 1-25/32 inches above the bottom of the blank. Also mark the position of the four locating dowels somewhere near the four corners of the blank.

Machining the blank

With the plane blank still on its side, drill 1/4-inch holes through the blank where the four locating pins go, and a 1/2-inch hole where the wedge pin goes.

At this point you should have a blank with five holes going all the way through it, and the 45-degree line and clearance angle lines drawn on it. I would transfer these marks onto the top and bottom of the plane so as not to lose them in subsequent operations.

With the plane blank resting on its bottom on the bandsaw table, bandsaw or resaw a 1/2-inch piece off each side. These

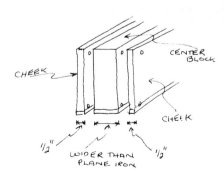

two 1/2-inch pieces are called the cheeks. This operation should leave a center block somewhat wider than your plane iron.

Thickness plane or joint to an even thickness the two cheeks to get out the unevenness left by the bandsaw.

Run one side of the center block over the jointer to get out

After the plane blank is glued up and the holes are drilled, the two cheeks are bandsawed off.

When bandsawing out the section of the center block, make sure you leave a feather of wood.

the bandsaw marks, and thickness plane the other side until the center block is 1/16 inch wider than your iron.

From the lines that you transferred onto the top and bottom of the blank, redraw the 45-degree angle line and clearance angle on the center block.

The next operation is to bandsaw out the section of the center block between the 45-degree angle line and the clearance-angle line. This middle piece (with the 1/2-inch hole in it) is the waste piece, and so the bandsawing must be on the waste side of the line. *Do not bandsaw through the bottom.* Rather, have the two bandsaw cuts meet exactly at the junction of the two lines, leaving a feather of wood connecting the two pieces which can be hinged and severed to separate the clearance-angle block from the 45-degree angle block.

If this is done properly, when the two cheeks are put back on and the locating pins put in, the resulting opening should be less than 1/32 inch. Also note not to discard the middle piece with the 1/2-inch hole. This will become the wedge.

At this point you can use any means at your disposal to clean up the surfaces of the 45-degree angle and the clearance angle. I prefer using a disk sander for the 45-degree angle, with the table set carefully at 90 degrees and a mitre gauge set at 45 degrees. To clean up a curved clearance angle, some kind of drum sander is helpful. Be careful to take away a minimum of material to prevent the opening from getting any wider than necessary.

A groove or slot must be made in the face of the 45-degree angle to allow for the cap screw on the chipbreaker. To determine how deep and how far down the face toward the opening it must be, you will have to take measurements from your iron and chipbreaker. The slot can be made with a gouge, router, chisel, horizontal boring machine, or any number of other methods you might have at your disposal.

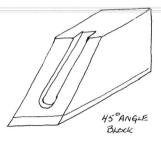

45° ANGLE BLOCK

Assembling and adjusting the plane

The pieces are now ready to glue back together. Have at the ready eight 1/4-inch locating pins about one inch long with chamfered ends, and plenty of clamps. The objective is to reassemble the plane blank as it was originally, save for the absence of the waste piece cut from the center block.

All in about five minutes time, spread glue on the same side of each of the 45-degree and clearance-angle blocks, position one cheek on, hammer in four of the pins, cut the

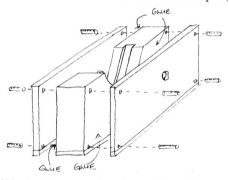

GLUE
GLUE GLUE

pins off flush (this makes clamping and handling easier), turn the assembly over, spread glue on the other side, position the second cheek, hammer in the pins, and cut them off flush; then clamp the whole works with as many clamps as possible, taking care to get tight glue joints on the sole.

Once the glue has set, unclamp and carefully clean all the excess glue out of the area inside the plane.

After sawing out the center, reglue the cheeks.

Plane all the locating dowels flush on both cheeks of the plane and lightly joint each side. Hopefully, if all has gone right, you should be able to slip the iron into the plane and it should *not* be able to come through the bottom.

Now, taking very light passes on the jointer, joint the plane bottom to widen the opening. When there is about 1/16 inch left to go before the iron can come through, *stop!* The rest will come off later with a little file.

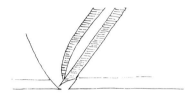

Sand the bottom carefully by placing a full sheet of fine sandpaper on a flat surface and rubbing the plane back and forth on it.

Before fitting the iron further, make a wedge out of the waste piece cut from the center block. It should not be so long that it blocks the shavings. It must also be narrow enough not

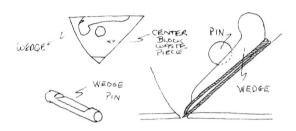

WEDGE

CENTER BLOCK WASTE PIECE

PIN

WEDGE PIN

WEDGE

to be too snug against the cheeks. Cut a length of 1/2-inch dowel for a wedge pin, making it as long as your plane is wide. File a flat on it wide enough to accommodate the wedge. Insert the pin with the flat down, but don't glue it.

Adjusting the opening

The adjustment of the opening is the most critical step in the making of a plane. The thing to remember is that you want the smallest opening that will still allow the shavings to pass freely. Using a small, fine needle file, file the leading edge of the opening at about 80 degrees to the bottom until the iron just slips through with no clearance to spare. Be

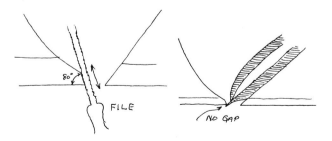

80°
FILE

NO GAP

careful, all the while, that the opening is even all the way across. At this point, a little bit more filing will begin to give the clearance needed to allow the shavings through. At this stage it's a good idea to seat the sharpened iron, chipbreaker and wedge, set the depth on the iron, and try a shaving or two.

(Adjust the iron down by light mallet taps on the back end. Adjust the tilt by tapping the sides of the iron. Bring the

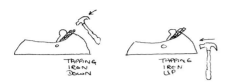

iron and wedge out by tapping the rear of the plane. The wedge should be tapped snug after adjusting the iron.)

If the shavings jam up in the opening, then it needs to be wider. Take the iron out, file a little more, and try again. You may have to do this half a dozen times.

When you finally get it right, take the iron out and chamfer the trailing edge of the opening. This will prevent it from getting chewed up. It does not affect the plane's function.

At this point you are on your own to modify and shape the plane to your own special design and use to fit your own hands and function. The only points to consider are that the rear of the iron should project slightly to allow easy tapping. (Most of the time I shorten the length of the iron so it does not project up too far.) And some provision should be made for tapping the iron and wedge up to remove them. A flat on the rear of the plane or a turned button there work well.

Remedying mistakes and defects

There are many little problems and mistakes that can be made but overcome.

If the opening is too wide, make a new sole and add it on. Or cut out a section of the sole in front of the opening and replace it with a larger piece to close up the opening. Or move the 45-degree angle block forward before the glue up. Or use a thicker iron.

If the iron is too wide for the plane, grind it narrower.

If the wedge or iron keeps slipping back, reduce the angle on the wedge, or roughen up the surface of the 45-degree angle block.

If the iron chatters when cutting, make the bottom side of the wedge concave to put more pressure down low on the iron.

In demonstrating plane-making to students, I have seen so many different ideas, shapes and methods of construction—most of which work beautifully—that I am convinced that the sky is the limit on how these planes can be made. Any number of planes can be made with modifications of the techniques described: molding, flat, round bottom, compass, block, bullnose, rabbeting, to name just a few. But that is a whole subject in itself. □

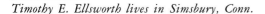

Timothy E. Ellsworth lives in Simsbury, Conn.

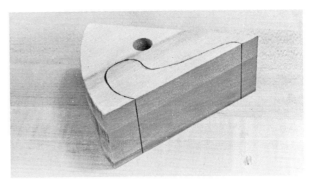

The section cut out of the center is a handy piece to use for the wedge. The precise shape is up to you.

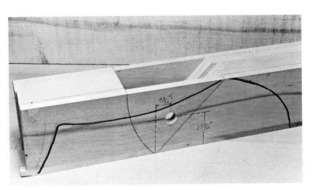

The plane is now ready for the critical adjustment of the opening using a jointer and needle file.

This is how the opening should look after it has been correctly filed. Chamfered trailing edge is not critical.

The finished plane, test shavings and all. Make the upper body shape whatever is most comfortable for you.

How to Make a Molding Plane
Sticking with an 18th-century tool

by Norman Vandal

You still can spot old molding planes in antique shops or junk shops, but they aren't as common as they used to be. Prices can be as low as $8 to $15, so people snap them up to use as decorations. I can see displaying these old tools because they are aesthetically pleasing, but it's really a shame not to fix them up and use them. They were fine tools once and can work just as well again.

I make a lot of period furniture, and I can't get along without my set of old planes. When I needed a reverse ogee molding with cove for a cornice on a cabinet, I decided to make a plane to do the job, designed around an old iron I'd found that had become separated from its original block.

I'll describe how to make such a plane from scratch, so that if you come across an old molding plane or iron you will be able to get it working again, regardless of its condition. Whether you are starting with an old plane block or an old iron, or from scratch, this is the general scheme: First you must know the molding profile, which will determine the width of the iron. Next you must shape the sole of the plane to the reverse profile of the molding. Then you can true the iron to the sole and start making molding.

If you come across a plane with a poorly shaped iron, don't change the shape of the sole to conform. The contour of the sole represents the molding the plane was designed to make. A poorly matched iron is usually the result of inept sharpen-ing or grinding. Recondition a damaged iron by annealing it (softening it by heating), filing it to fit the sole and then re-tempering it.

The style of plane I've chosen is based on the finer 18th-century examples, and all the standard dimensions discussed are characteristic of this period. You may, of course, alter the design, but this pattern is a good starting point.

Molding shapes—Planes with an average length of 9 in. to 10 in., a height of 3 in., a thickness of from 1 in. to 2½ in. and no handle have erroneously been accepted as "molding planes." Many of these planes are for rabbeting, tongue-and-grooving, dadoing and other purposes that have nothing to do with making moldings. Molding planes produce moldings on the edges of frame members called sticks, hence the process is called sticking. Figure 1 shows some standard mold-ings, and the bibliography at the end of this article includes books that contain full-size drawings.

Simple moldings (composed of segments of circles or el-lipses) are beads, quarter rounds, hollows and rounds, coves or scotias, and astragal beads. Planes for making these profiles are called simple molding planes. Complex moldings, often broken up or set off by flats or fillets, are ogees, reverse ogees, ovolos or compositions of various curves. Planes to stick these shapes are called complex molding planes. There is another

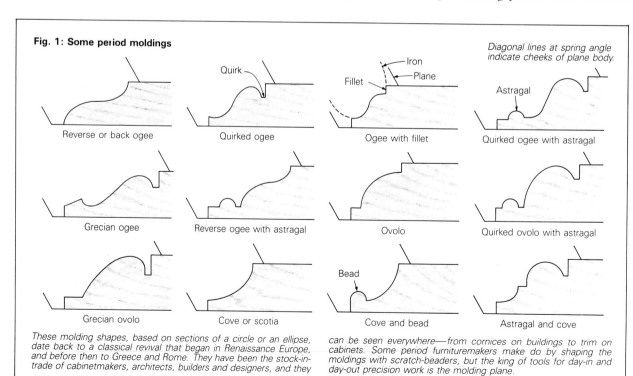

Fig. 1: Some period moldings

Quirk

Fillet — Iron
— Plane

Diagonal lines at spring angle indicate cheeks of plane body.

Astragal

Reverse or back ogee   Quirked ogee   Ogee with fillet   Quirked ogee with astragal

Grecian ogee   Reverse ogee with astragal   Ovolo   Quirked ovolo with astragal

Grecian ovolo   Cove or scotia   Bead   Cove and bead   Astragal and cove

These molding shapes, based on sections of a circle or an ellipse, date back to a classical revival that began in Renaissance Europe, and before then to Greece and Rome. They have been the stock-in-trade of cabinetmakers, architects, builders and designers, and they can be seen everywhere—from cornices on buildings to trim on cabinets. Some period furnituremakers make do by shaping the moldings with scratch-beaders, but the king of tools for day-in and day-out precision work is the molding plane.

The plane shown above began with an old iron. Vandal annealed and reshaped the iron, then made a yellow-birch block to suit. In the photo sequence below, the plane is tilted, or sprung, so the fence will be pressed against the work. A series of passes then takes progressively wider shavings, until the depth stop contacts the work, and the plane ceases to cut.

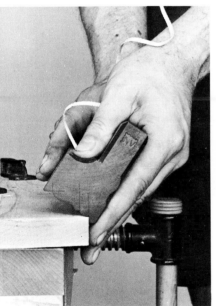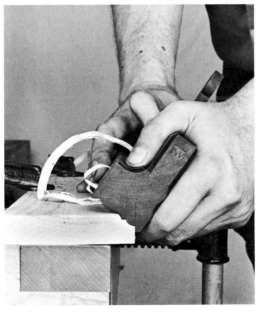

class of planes generally used to cut wider moldings. These planes are from 12 in. to 14 in. long, and have a throat, wedge system and handle similar to common bench planes. They have been dubbed "crown molding planes," though this type of plane cuts many sorts of moldings other than crowns or cornices.

The design—The first step in making any molding plane is choosing the molding. Draw its section full-size, and refine the drawing before beginning the plane. Simple planes can make moldings up to about 2½ in. wide. Wider moldings will have to be made with more than one plane, or with a crown molding plane.

Use the molding section to construct a full-size drawing of the heel, or rear, of the plane, as this will settle the size of the

block needed. The sole of any molding plane is the reverse profile of the molding it cuts, plus the integral fence and the depth stop. Looking at my plane from the rear, the fence is on the left and the depth stop on the right (figure 2, top of next page).

In use, the stock is fastened horizontally to the bench and the plane is tilted, or "sprung," so that the fence is vertical and the depth stop horizontal, as shown in the photos above. An unsprung plane can wander, but a sprung plane gives greater control because the guide fence is pressed against the stock. The plane, even though tilted, cuts straight down the side of the work, gradually taking a wider and wider shaving until the full profile has been stuck. When the depth stop contacts the top of the work, the iron stops cutting. Not only is a sprung plane easier to use, but its geometry will also

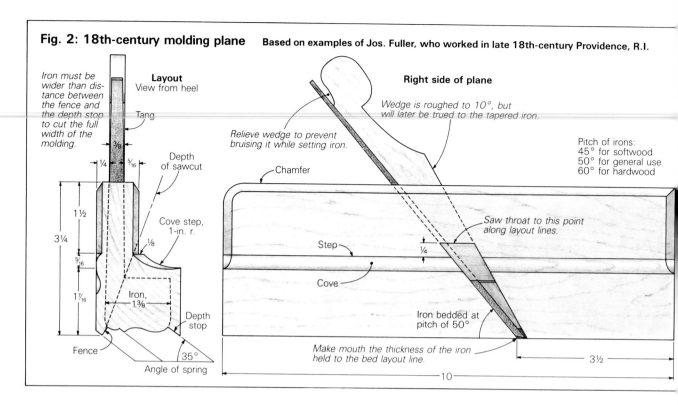

Fig. 2: 18th-century molding plane Based on examples of Jos. Fuller, who worked in late 18th-century Providence, R.I.

Iron must be wider than distance between the fence and the depth stop to cut the full width of the molding.

Layout View from heel

Tang

⅜

¼   ⁵⁄₁₆

Depth of sawcut

1½

3¼   Cove step, 1-in. r.

⅛

⁵⁄₁₆

1⁷⁄₁₆

Iron, 1⅜

Depth stop

Fence

35°

Angle of spring

Right side of plane

Wedge is roughed to 10°, but will later be trued to the tapered iron.

Relieve wedge to prevent bruising it while setting iron.

Chamfer

Pitch of irons:
45° for softwood
50° for general use
60° for hardwood

Saw throat to this point along layout lines.

Step

¼

Cove

Iron bedded at pitch of 50°

Make mouth the thickness of the iron held to the bed layout line.

3½

10

allow its mouth to be more uniform in width (figure 3, top of facing page). Not all 18th-century molders were sprung, however, and a sprung plane won't cut some molding shapes.

Draw the molding with the appropriate spring, which can vary—good working angles are shown in figure 1. Then add the fence and depth stop to the molding profile. I allow ¼ in. on the fence side, and ⁵⁄₁₆ in. on the depth-stop side. Your drawing now shows the total width of the plane.

The top of a molding plane is stepped down in thickness. The width of the stepped portion will be the width of the iron's tang plus ¼ in. at the left and ⁵⁄₁₆ in. at the right. The extra width makes up for the wood that will be cut from the throat. You can judge from figure 2 the height of a typical step.

The stock—Yellow birch was used by 18th-century plane-makers, but by the turn of the 19th century beech had become the wood of choice. I prefer quartersawn yellow birch, but beech, maple or cherry will work as well. Select as fine a block of wood as you can—straight-grained and consistent throughout. Avoid figured wood, or you'll have problems shaping the sole.

My rough block length for a 10-in. long plane is 12 in., which gives me an inch at each end to experiment with when shaping the sole profile, and also allows for cutting off bruises inflicted during shaping. The finished height of most blocks is about 3¼ in. Standard dimensions meant planes could be stored and transported in fitted boxes without rattling around.

The iron—Since I figure that I'll use any molding shape sooner or later, I frequently buy old irons that have lost their blocks, then make new blocks to fit. I've had some good luck, but looking for a usable iron that's also a shape you need can be futile, so I recommend that you make your own.

The easiest way to make an iron is to start with a piece of dead-soft sheet tool steel, work it with a file and hacksaw,

and then temper it after shaping. Alternatively, you can have a blacksmith forge an iron out of spring steel, which can be annealed and shaped, then tempered as a last step. Hayrake tines and old buggy springs forge into excellent irons.

Iron thickness can be from ⅛ in. to ³⁄₁₆ in. The thicker irons will chatter less, but will be more difficult to shape. Old plane irons were tapered in thickness. A light tap on the end of the tang would loosen a tapered iron slightly while driving it deeper into the block. Then a sharp tap on the wedge could secure the iron without altering the set. The tapered iron, while nice to have, is not a necessity. And a uniformly thick iron is much simpler to make. Keep in mind that the iron must be wider than the cutting portion of the sole—if the profile ends at the side of the iron, you won't be able to set the iron deep enough to cut the full width of the molding.

Layout—When your block is planed and trued square, lay out the cuts and mortises. Start by making a full-size template of the sole profile, directly from the full-size drawing of the molding. To make the template, I use aluminum flashing. It is easy to work, and the edges of the template remain crisp during tracing. Position the template in the same place on each end of the block and trace the sole profile.

Next, lay out the throat, mouth and wedge slot using the dimensions given in figure 2. I suggest a 50° pitch for the iron—a compromise for cutting either hard or soft woods. The wood which the iron rests against is called the bed. The opposite side of the mortise will be cut at an angle 10° greater, to allow for the wedge taper. Carry the layout lines all around the body of the plane to define the mouth opening and the tang mortise on top of the block. Lay out the mortise width according to the width of the tang.

Last, use a marking gauge to scribe the step. The step makes the plane easier to handle, helps the shaving out of the throat, and makes cutting the mortise for the wedge and iron

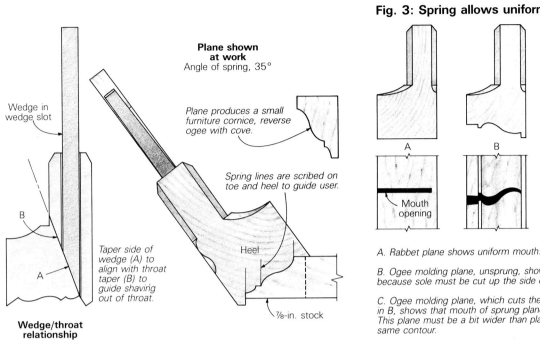

Wedge in
wedge slot

**Plane shown
at work**
Angle of spring, 35°

*Plane produces a small
furniture cornice, reverse
ogee with cove.*

B

A

*Taper side of
wedge (A) to
align with throat
taper (B) to
guide shaving
out of throat.*

*Spring lines are scribed on
toe and heel to guide user.*

Heel

⁷⁄₈-in. stock

**Wedge/throat
relationship**

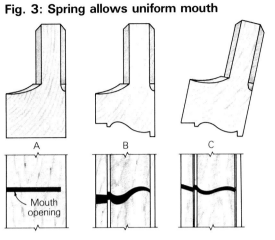

Fig. 3: Spring allows uniform mouth

A   B   C

Mouth
opening

A. Rabbet plane shows uniform mouth.

B. Ogee molding plane, unsprung, shows irregular mouth
because sole must be cut up the side of the plane.

C. Ogee molding plane, which cuts the same molding as
in B, shows that mouth of sprung plane remains uniform.
This plane must be a bit wider than plane B to cut the
same contour.

*An intricate sole can be shaped by a series of cove and straight
cuts on the tablesaw, and then sanded with shaped blocks.*

Boxing the sole

Slivers of Turkish boxwood can be let into the sole of a
plane to reinforce it at points where use would wear it
down. Boxwood—the familiar yellow wood used in old
Stanley folding rules—is dense, tight-grained and extremely
wear-resistant.

Planemakers plowed narrow grooves into the sole of the
plane, inserted thin slips of boxwood, then trued up the
sole. In order to make the slips even more wear-resistant,
makers set the grain of the boxwood nearly at right angles
to that of the plane body, so that the tougher end grain was
exposed to take the abuses.

Boxing was not common in 18th-century planes, but it
caught on fast—it is found in almost all molding planes
produced after the turn of the 19th century.   —N.V.

easier, as we shall see. The edge of the step can be decorated
in a number of ways—molded with ogee or quarter-round
profiles, chamfered, or simply beveled off. I decorate my steps
by cutting a cove the full length of the plane. Lay out the
decoration now, too.

Shaping the sole and step—Period planemakers duplicated
many profile molders. Instead of shaping each sole with files
and gouges, they devised a "mother plane," made in reverse
profile, to stick each profile. The mother plane saved time,
and it ensured that all the planes for a specific molding would
be the same, at least those from any one workshop. I've never
bothered to make a mother plane, though, because I've never
needed more than one plane of each shape.

Cut the sole and the step decoration prior to sawing out
the mouth and throat—these gaps would interfere with the
shaping. It's vital that the sole be uniform from end to end,
or you won't be able to set the iron properly. Various tools
and techniques can be used to shape the sole. For the fence
and depth stop, or any other flat portions of the profile, I use
the tablesaw to make cuts the full length of the sole.

The concave areas can be gouged and filed, or cut on a
router table using various cove or fluting bits. By making a
number of repeated cuts, not quite to the layout line, you can
remove most of the material. The sole can then be scraped or
sanded smooth, with the sandpaper wrapped around a dowel.
For shaping convex areas I generally use hollow planes, but
other methods work too. Again you can remove most of the
material using router or tablesaw, then clean up with chisels,
scrapers and a shaped sanding block.

Check the sole with a straightedge, and then true any hollows or high spots.

The steps on period planes were probably cut with a large
rabbet or fillister plane—chatter marks from the iron are often
visible. I cut the step on the tablesaw and scrape the surfaces

smooth, saving the waste to make the wedge. At this point you can cut the decoration on the step.

Sawing out the mouth

Sawing out the mouth—Surprisingly, a good deal of the mouth and wedge slot can be made by simply sawing out the area between the layout lines. Mark out how far up the body of the plane you wish to saw. This cut is a compromise between leaving enough wood above the step for strength and providing a gentle angle to guide the shaving out of the throat. I usually stop the sawcuts ¼ in. above the step.

Figure 2 shows how deep to cut across the sole. I use a miter box to start the cuts at the proper angles for the blade and the wedge—the miter box also ensures that the throat will begin straight across the sole. I use the backsaw freehand to finish the cuts.

The wood between the kerfs can now be chiseled out, and pared as smooth as possible. You will find that a ⅛-in. chisel is a great help in clearing out the mouth.

Mortising the wedge slot

Mortising the wedge slot—The angled mortises in period planes were, I believe, chopped out without pre-boring—production planemakers of yesteryear had plenty of practice. I find it a lot safer to pre-bore the wedge slot with a bit slightly smaller than the width of the mortise, using a guideblock bored at the correct angle. A drill press could be used, or any number of jigs worked out. It's important to bore accurately, without cutting into either the bed or wedge ends of the mortise. Bore all the way through to the throat.

Now pare the sides and ends down to the layout lines. Some chopping is required, but don't rush it—many a plane has been spoiled at this point. You have to chisel the wedge end of the mortise into end grain at a 40° angle. Patience and an absolutely sharp chisel will prevail.

After my wedge-slot mortise has been cut, I use a set of planemaker's floats (see article, page 46) to true up the bed and the mortise. Floats are single-cut files of various shapes and sizes with widely spaced teeth, each of which functions like a tiny chisel. Original floats are extremely scarce, and command high prices. I have a set that a friend made me on his milling machine, and I value them highly. Although they make truing up a lot easier, floats aren't strictly necessary—careful paring with a chisel can produce as good a result.

The width of the mortise isn't crucial, just make sure there is adequate clearance for the iron without removing too much wood. The bed, however, must be perfectly flat—or the iron will chatter. For the final fitting, use your iron to check out the bed surface, the mortise width and the mouth. But check the iron itself for flatness first. The wedge end of the mortise must also be flat, and square to the plane's sides.

Much of the angled mortise can be started with a backsaw and then pared away, but the inside should be drilled and chopped.

The plane's wedge is made from the scrap left over when the step was cut. Its lower end will be tapered to guide the shaving out.

Making the wedge

Making the wedge—Take the cutoff you saved when you made the step, and thickness it to the width of the tang. Taper it to 10° so it will fit the mortise. I make the angled cut with a fine-tooth handsaw and plane it true and smooth with a block plane. Now set the iron in the plane and insert the wedge against it with the grain of the wood parallel to the iron. The wedge must fit tight to hold the iron firmly against the bed, and to prevent shavings from catching between the wedge and iron, jamming up the mouth and throat. Carefully pare away wood from the mortise until you get a perfect fit.

Shaping the iron

Shaping the iron—The blank has to be annealed, so that it can be worked to shape, then rehardened. To anneal the iron, you can use a propane torch, or better yet a hotter MAPP gas torch, heating the iron to a dull red glow, then letting it cool slowly for an hour or two. If the steel is properly annealed you should be able to cut it with a file or hacksaw.

Once you've shaped the tang so the iron fits neatly in the plane, the cutting edge can be laid out to the shape of the sole. This must be done while the iron is set flat on the bed. I make a full-size template of the iron out of aluminum flashing. Place the template in the plane as a substitute iron, holding it tightly in place with the wedge and making sure that its full width protrudes slightly beyond the sole. Using a sharp marking awl, scribe the contour of the sole on the underside of the template. Remove the template and cut out the traced profile with a tin snips or knife. The line of the cutting edge must pass into the body of the plane at the fence and depth stop—carry this line out to the sides of the template. This will not give you an entirely exact profile for the cutting edge, but it's as close as you can come at this point.

Next, paint the bottom inch of the wedge side of the iron with either machinists' blue layout dye or flat black paint. When this is dry, lay the aluminum template on it and, using the awl, scribe the cutting edge's contour. You can use a grinder for roughing out, but a file will give you the greatest accuracy for the final cuts to the scribed line. Place the iron in a vise, paint side toward you, and go at it. Don't worry about the bevel of the iron yet, just file square to the contour.

Now turn the underside of the iron toward you to file the

bevel: all but the cutting edge itself must clear the sole. Thus the bevel angle is dependent upon the angle at which the iron is bedded, the pitch. For a plane with 50° pitch I give the iron at least a 55° bevel (a 5° clearance angle), which usually proves sufficient. Set a bevel square to the bevel angle and file up to the cutting edge.

When the edge is formed, position the iron with the wedge in the plane, so that the iron protrudes about 1/32 in. Check for clearance, and sight down the sole of the plane from toe to heel to see that the iron protrudes uniformly. Remove the iron and touch it up with a file where necessary.

When everything is right, remove all traces of the paint or layout dye. File all parts of the bevel as smooth as you can, because once the iron is tempered, a file will not easily cut the steel. Next, polish the iron. I use a muslin wheel charged with gray compound (tripoli). The shiny, buffed surface will allow you to see the colors of the steel—your clue to the correct temperatures—while you temper the iron.

Tempering—I confess I have little scientific knowledge of tempering. I learned from a local blacksmith who was even less scientific than myself. I don't have my own forge, but a MAPP gas torch works quite well on small pieces such as plane irons. Heat the iron until it glows dark cherry red in dim light. This is about 1550°F to 1600°F. Don't direct the flame at the cutting edge—the edge reaches a hotter temperature anyhow, and there's no sense in burning it. When the color is right, plunge the iron vertically into a pail of cool, salted water. When cool, the iron will be in the hard state. Buff it until it shines again, and test it with a file.

Next, temper the iron by heating it until the polished surface turns a light straw color. This will be about 500°F to 600°F—nowhere near as hot as when heating to harden. When the color is right, plunge the iron into the water. Then check it for hardness with a file, which should be barely able to cut. If it isn't hard enough, start over.

Buff the tempered iron clean, and use a set of Arkansas slip stones to hone the tricky spots. Use plenty of lubricating oil until the entire bevel gleams.

Finishing the wedge—With the rough wedge against the iron in the plane, mark the wedge's decorative profile. Then shape the wedge on the bandsaw or scroll saw, and sand the edges smooth. The wedge in figure 2 is typical of a prolific 18th-century planemaker, Joseph Fuller, of Providence, R.I.

Taper the tip of the wedge to allow the shaving to escape the mouth and be directed up and out of the throat. The tip will sometimes have to be cut back a little. Taper from the end up to the bottom of the angled mortise—if the taper extends into the mortise you will trap shavings.

After chamfering and carving some decoration on the block, I stain the yellow birch and apply three coats of Minwax antique oil as a sealer and final finish. The plane is now about ready to go to work.

Setting the iron—Place the iron in the plane and insert the wedge loosely. Sighting down the sole from the rear of the

---

Norman Vandal, of Roxbury, Vt., makes period architectural components in the summertime and period furniture during the winter.

plane, set the iron so the cutting edge is just shy of the mouth, and drive the wedge, but not as tight as it will be during use. It helps to have a light positioned behind you, to reflect off the bevel as it protrudes. Get the final set by tapping the end of the iron, then drive the wedge tight. Use a mallet on the wedge and a ball peen or other small hammer on the iron. To loosen the wedge, hold the plane in your left hand and give the heel a sharp blow with the mallet. Be careful the iron doesn't fall out of the mouth of the plane.

Lubricate the sole to minimize friction and to prevent pitch buildup. Cabinetmakers used to use tallow, kept in cups fastened beneath their benches. I use paste wax, and sometimes mineral oil, though mineral oil tends to darken the sole.

Depending on the wood and the amount of set, it might take twenty to forty passes to stick your molding. Start with the plane sprung so the fence is flat against the edge of the board. Keep pressure against the fence with each pass, and be sure to keep the spring lines vertical, otherwise the molding may end up with a tilt.

Making wooden planes in the old manner is an all-but-forgotten trade. I hope you will be inspired to give it a try—to experience the immense pleasure of using a tool you have restored or, better still, designed and built on your own. □

A molding plane can yield a crisp, traditional molding, free of machine-tool marks and needing no sanding.

Further reading
Wooden Planes in 19th-Century America, Kenneth Roberts, Kenneth Roberts Publishing Co., Fitzwilliam, N.H., volumes one and two. Note: Volume two features the most comprehensive material ever published on making wooden planes.
Dictionary of Tools Used in the Woodworking and Allied Trades, R.A. Salaman, Charles Scribner's Sons, New York, 1975. Includes planemakers' tools and the processes involved.
Alex Mathieson & Sons, 1899 Woodworking Tools, a catalog reprint, Kenneth Roberts, Kenneth Roberts Publishing Co., Fitzwilliam, N.H. Many full-size drawings of period moldings.
Chapin-Stephens Catalog No. 114, 1901, a catalog reprint, Kenneth Roberts, Kenneth Roberts Publishing Co., Fitzwilliam, N.H. Molding planes in sticking positions; useful for designing.
Explanation or Key, to the Various Manufactories of Sheffield, Joseph Smith, 1816, a reprint by Early American Industries Assn., South Burlington, Vt., 1975. Historical information.
Woodworking Planes, a Descriptive Register of Wooden Planes, Alvin Sellens, Augusta, Kans., 1978. A valuable compilation.

Q & A

Caring for tools in a cold shop—*Like many craftsmen, I've invested a good deal of money in power and hand tools. My equipment is kept in the garage, which doubles as my workshop. I heat the garage only when I'm woodworking and I've noticed that when I bring a cold tool into the house, it seems to get damp and I'm worried that my tools will be damaged by rust. Any suggestions?*
—*William A. Schmitt, Chicago, Ill.*

SIMON WATTS REPLIES: The heat in my shop is on only when I'm there during the winter. The temperature drops well below zero. The machines groan a bit when you first start them up but as soon as the lubricant in the bearings warms up, they run normally. Rapid changes in temperature and humidity can produce condensation, but it shouldn't be a big problem if you don't make a habit of taking tools and machines into a warm and humid house. The problem I have with cold workshops is the freezing of glue and paints. White and yellow glues are no good after they've been frozen and latex paints turn to a useless curdle after three or four freeze cycles. Consequently, I keep these items in the house until I'm ready to use them.

RICHARD STARR REPLIES: If you wipe your tools off quickly when you bring them into the house, a little condensation shouldn't hurt them. I don't see a cold garage being as harmful to tools as a damp basement can be. Summer's humidity condenses on the cool walls and on everything else in the room and when that happens, you've got a serious problem. The best solution I've found is to spray tools with a light mist of WD-40, a non-greasy, water-absorbent lubricant available from auto supply stores. It won't harm finished or unfinished wooden parts, and an occasional application will prevent rust.

Protecting tools from rust—*A couple of years ago I purchased a six-piece Swiss carving set from a mail-order company. A while back, I noticed they were getting patches of rust on them, even the ones I don't use. I thought about putting oil on them to stop the rust but I'm afraid the protective coating will spoil my carvings. How can I clean and preserve these tools between use? How should I store these tools to protect them?*
—*George Adams, Louisville, Ohio*

A bit of fine steel wool should knock off any rust spots on your tools. After you have done that, you could treat them with a rust-preventive spray, or wrap them in protective paper. One type of spray is available from Schwab Industries, Inc., PO Box 1269, Sequim, Wash. 98382. Protective paper is made by Brauer Bros., 2012 Washington, St. Louis, Mo. 63103. Even after treatment, the tools will hold up better if they are stored in a dry tool cabinet.

Old planes—*I have three sets of wooden tongue-and-groove planes. None of these planes cuts the tongue or the groove in the center of the stock thickness. The tongue and the groove match, and the boards fit together, but the joint is off-center. Is this the way these planes were intended to cut? Also, I'd like to know what the purpose of the flat spot is on some molding planes I have. Is this used as a guide to cut the molding?* —*Bob Vinas, Bayside, N.Y.*

NORMAN VANDAL REPLIES: There are two reasons why many wooden match planes were designed to cut the tongue and groove off-center. When tongue-and-groove boards were used

as flooring, or in other applications where surface wear was a consideration, placing the groove farther from the face of the board allowed more wood to wear away before the joint was exposed. Second, the edges of tongue-and-groove boards used in wainscoting, paneling, or cabinet construction were often decorated with a bead as in the drawing below. An off-center joint left enough material on the finished face so that this bead could be cut without weakening or exposing the joint.

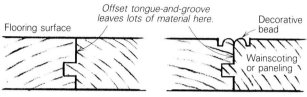

The flat you describe is commonly found on planes called hollows and rounds. These were sold in pairs: one cuts a concave and the other a convex segment of the same size circle. These planes have a number on the heel which indicates size, and were often sold in sets of nine pairs, numbered evenly from 2 to 18. There were no universal standards, however, so a number 6, say, from one maker will not necessarily be the same size as a number 6 from a different maker.

Hollows and rounds, having no fence to control the location or depth of the cut, are held freehand. The flat can serve as a guide when run along a fence clamped to the work, but its real purpose was just to shear off the side of the plane body. This exposes the iron along the edge, so the plane can cut all the way into a tight corner.

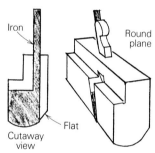

To get satisfactory results from these planes, you'll need to tune them. They tend to warp, especially around the mouth. Sight down the sole from toe to heel, with the iron removed, and note any inconsistencies. The sole of the plane must be straight, so correct any problems with a file and sandpaper. True up the iron so that it protrudes evenly at all points along the cutting edge. Now you're ready to go.

Stanley R&L Co—*At a recent garage sale, I purchased several old tools including two planes marked Stanley #605 and #608. After cleaning the #608, a 24-in. jointer with a corrugated sole, I noticed the inscription "PATD APR 2 '95" on the body and "STANLEY R&L CO." on the frog. What does the R&L stand for? Also, has anyone published a list and description of all the models of planes produced by Stanley?* —*Bart Wesley, Denison, Tex.*

The R&L stands for Stanley Rule and Level Co. There are several lists of the old Stanley planes, a number of reprints of old Stanley catalogs and a few organizations of collectors of old tools. You should start by getting in touch with the Early American Industries Association, Old Economy, Ambridge, Pa. 15003. This is the national organization of collectors and users of old tools, with lots of local chapters, a quarterly journal and a newsletter. Then there is the British-American Rhykenological Society, 60 Harvest Lane, Levittown, N.Y. 11756. Rhykenology is the study of planes. Finally, Roger K. Smith at 1444 N. Main St., Lancaster, Mass. 01523 sells reprints of Stanley's illustrated 1909 catalog.

A Pair of Panel-Raising Planes
Two is more than twice as good

by Robert Bourdeau

In a recent project, a Louis XV armoire for my daughter, I used the shaper to raise the many panels for the doors and case sides. I was disappointed with the results—especially with tear-out both across and along the grain. Quite a bit of sanding was required to eliminate the pits and gouges; further, the crisp look and feel of cleanly cut wood was gone.

When it came time for me to begin work on my son's roll-top desk, and I wanted to raise its panels with double bevels, I discovered that the appropriate shaper knives would have to be custom-ground at a high cost. There had to be a better way, so I decided to make myself a pair of panel-raising planes, a left-hand and right-hand, which would allow me to plane in the direction of the grain regardless of the side of the panel I might be working on. This meant that I could keep tear-out and splintering under control, minimizing the amount of sanding I'd have to do.

I had never made a plane before, but after studying K.D. Roberts' *Wooden Planes in 19th Century America* and reading about paneled doors and walls (in *Fine Woodworking* magazine) and Timothy Ellsworth's "Hand Planes" (page 24), I felt I could make the pair of panel-raising planes by laminating the bodies. I began with a full-

Tear-out from planing against the grain, always a problem when using a single panel-raising plane, is minimized by having two, a left-hand and a right-hand model. No matter how the grain runs, one plane or the other can follow it.

Photos: Yvon Bourdeau

scale sectional drawing of the panel I wanted (figure 1); the double bevel would form a tongue on the panel's edge and make for a nicer fit in the frame grooves than would an unrelieved wedge. Using ¾-in. stock, I divided the thickness of the panel into even thirds and decided to cut a ¼-in. by ⅜-in. rabbet along the back edge of each panel to form the back side of the ¼-in. tongue. When captured in the grooves, there's a resulting ⅛-in. wide gap between the vertical shoulder of this rabbet and the inner edges of the frame. This means that the panel can expand a full ¼ in. before it exerts any pressure against the frame, a sufficient allowance for most panels, unless they are exceptionally wide or made from an unstable wood. For a pleasing appearance, the back edges of the panel can be chamfered or slightly rounded over, as can the inner edges of the frame.

Since the profile of the panel's field, shoulder and bevel is the exact complement of the plane's sole, it was an easy matter to draw the plane in section atop the panel (figure 2) just as though the plane were making its final pass down the edge. By laminating the body of the plane with two sides, or cheeks, and a three-part core (a front block, an adjustable shoe and a rear block), the task of shaping the sole to the required angles was made much easier and simpler than would have been the case had I tried to make the entire body from a solid block in the traditional way. I beveled the bottom of the inside cheek at 6° off perpendicular and did the same to the outside cheek, the only difference between the two being that the outside cheek projects below the sole, while the inside cheek does not. See figure 2 for an elevation view of these parts. This arrangement determines the angle of the bevel and the final depth of cut, though these can be varied by altering the thickness of the shim, which is clamped to the bench along the edge of the panel and which stops the cut when the bottom edge of the outside cheek contacts it.

I set the two cheeks aside and turned to making the blank for the three core pieces. I laminated the blank from face-glued lengths of ½-in. thick maple. When the glue was dry, I dimensioned the blank 14 in. long by 2¼ in. high by 1¹³⁄₁₆ in. wide, this last dimension being final and the other two slightly oversize. Since a ¼-in. strip along the outside edge of the sole must be beveled at 6°, I set my jointer fence at 84° and took a few light passes until the jointed surface was exactly ¼ in. wide. This is the part of the sole that conforms to the second bevel, the face side of the tongue.

I reasoned that the iron should be skewed at 30° in the body of the plane and that its cutting angle should be 35°, though 45° is common on traditional planes of this type. This meant that the face of the rear block that would support the iron would have to be cut on a compound angle as shown in figure 4—60° in the horizontal plane, 35° in the vertical. You can make this cut by angling the miter gauge and tilting the arbor on the table saw, or by setting up the radial-arm saw for cutting a compound angle. From the toe of the angle to the rear of the blank should be about 9 in. You must orient the blank correctly when cutting; its 1¹³⁄₁₆-in. width is a finished dimension. The height and length will be trimmed after the body is glued up. The inner face of the forward block must also be cut at a compound angle—120° in the horizontal plane (to complement the 60° skew angle of the rear block) and 65° in the vertical plane. Since the core blank is about ³⁄₁₆ in. too high, you can rip off a ¾-in. thick slice from the beveled sole to produce the adjustable shoe. Make a

smooth cut, so that the sawn surfaces will mate uniformly.

As a final step before gluing up the body, cut a ½-in. wide tapered dado in the inside cheek about 1 in. forward of the mouth. I also cut a ½-in. wide dado ³⁄₃₂ in. deep in the corresponding place on the side of the forward core block. When the parts were glued together these two dadoes formed the tapered slot for the scribing spur and its wedge. The purpose of the spur, which I made from a length of ordinary hacksaw blade, is to score the wood in advance of the cutter when planing across the grain, thus to eliminate tearing the stock.

Now the body can be glued up (with the movable shoe left out). Be sure to position the rear and forward blocks so that if the angled face of the forward block were extended, it would intersect the face of the rear block at the surface of the sole. The acute angle on the adjustable shoe will be pared back at a later time to make room for the extended iron (figure 4, detail A). And the throat opening can always be enlarged by adjusting the shoe. Be careful about positioning the cheeks in relation to the core blocks when gluing up. You may want to use pins to help locate the parts and to keep them from swimming out of alignment under clamping pressure.

When the glue has set, plane the top edges of the core blocks flush with the top surfaces of the cheeks. The movable shoe is secured by means of a ¼-in. machine screw that passes through a slotted hole (⅜ in. by ¼ in.) in the forward block and screws into a T-nut set in a plugged counterbore in the shoe. You can make the slotted hole easily by boring two ¼-in. dia. holes and chiseling out the waste between. The washer can either be let into the block or sit proud of the surface.

I made the handle to fit my hand and working posture. The angle between the handle and the body of the plane (and also its point of attachment) determines how efficiently your muscular energy is transmitted to the cutting edge, so it's a good idea to experiment with several angles and shapes before making a final decision on the handle design that's correct for you. The handle is attached to the body by a long ¼-in. screw or bolt that extends through a hole bored through the full length of the handle and is screwed into a T-nut in the rear block. This T-nut, like the one in the movable shoe, is retained in a plugged counterbore.

The cutter has to be ground to conform exactly with the profile of the sole. This is critical. To ensure this conformity, I inserted the iron blank in the body and traced the profile of the sole with layout dye onto the steel and then traced again with a sharp machinist's scribe. I used a jig for grinding (see photo on page 40) and I made periodic checks, re-inserting the iron into the body, to make certain the shape was being properly formed. I ground the bevel on the iron to 30°, which provided a clearance angle of 5°.

I made the chip breaker from ⅛-in. mild steel, which I first hacksawed and then filed to the final shape that is shown in figure 3. I used a small, round file to form the groove across the face of the chip breaker where it bears against the steel retaining pin. I drilled and tapped the upper part of the chip breaker to receive a ¼-in. thumbscrew. A square, steel pressure plate, countersunk to receive the end of the thumbscrew, presses against the iron when the screw is tightened. Even greater pressure is levered against the toe of the chip breaker where it contacts the iron just above the cutting edge. You may want to use the traditional wedge here, which should exert uniform pressure along the length of the iron.

The iron should be ¹⁄₁₆ in. narrower than the opening in

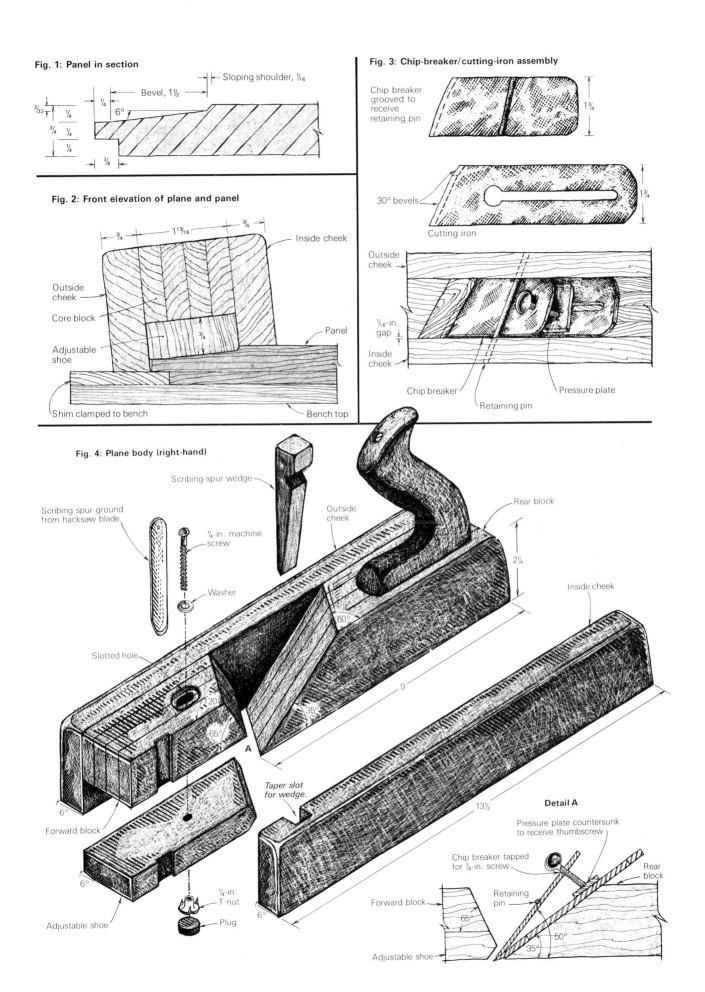

Fig. 1: Panel in section

Sloping shoulder, 1/16

Bevel, 1½

6°

3/32 1/4
3/4 1/4
1/4
3/8

Fig. 2: Front elevation of plane and panel

3/4 1 13/16 3/4

Inside cheek

Outside cheek

Core block

Adjustable shoe

3/4

Panel

Shim clamped to bench

Bench top

Fig. 3: Chip-breaker/cutting-iron assembly

Chip breaker grooved to receive retaining pin

1¾

30° bevels

Cutting iron

1¾

Outside cheek

1/16-in. gap

Inside cheek

Chip breaker

Retaining pin

Pressure plate

Fig. 4: Plane body (right-hand)

Scribing-spur wedge

Scribing spur ground from hacksaw blade

¼-in. machine screw

Washer

Outside cheek

Rear block

2¼

Inside cheek

Slotted hole

20

65°

35

9

A

6°

Forward block

6°

Adjustable shoe

Taper slot for wedge.

¼-in. T-nut

Plug

60°

13½

6°

Detail A

Pressure plate countersunk to receive thumbscrew

Chip breaker tapped for ¼-in. screw

Forward block

Retaining pin

65°

Rear block

50°

35°

Adjustable shoe

Planes and Chisels **39**

Author's grinding jig holds the iron at a fixed angle (top photo), yet its base is unattached, allowing the profile to be shaped freehand. In raising the panel, the plane is first canted to the outside to take several narrow shavings (center photo). Then it's canted to the inside for several passes, and then several cuts are taken down the middle of the bevel. Only when making the last two or three passes is a cut taken the full width of the iron (bottom photo). This method reduces the chance of tearing the grain and is less tiring than taking a full cut with each pass.

which it rests, and it should fit snugly against the inside of the outside cheek. This leaves a 1/16-in. gap between the iron and the inside cheek, which makes room for the sloped shoulder to be formed. Looking back at figure 2, you will see a small triangular space between the edge of the panel and the inner edge of the outside cheek. Imagine the plane just beginning to make its first pass along the flat edge of the panel. The plane's body would be oriented at 90° to the panel's surface. With each successive pass and the removal of a single shaving, the plane's body cants more and more to the outside of the panel, and with each pass the cutting toe of the iron changes its attitude and its distance from the original shoulder line. The triangular space between cheek and panel edge widens and deepens as the bevel is cut. As the plane's body cants and the iron is pulled more to the outside, the sloping shoulder is formed.

I ground the scribing spur to a round-nose shape only after experimenting with several other cutting configurations. The round-nose spur need not be inclined forward in the body as shown in the photos. Care must be taken to set the spur at the exact depth of the iron. If set even slightly deeper than the iron, it will leave ugly lines in the sloped shoulder; if set higher than the iron, it will not sever the tissue through to the depth of cut, and tear-out and splintering could result.

The left-hand plane is made exactly like the right-hand one, only everything is reversed as in a mirror. The iron, of course, must be ground to precisely the same profile as on the other plane, as you may very well be planing the same bevel with both planes, since the grain direction can reverse in the middle of a board.

In use, I have learned that long, uninterrupted strokes are best, beginning at one end and going right through to the other. The outside cheek should always be kept snug against the edge of the panel when planing. To save your strength and to proceed at a workmanlike pace, begin cutting first to the outside, removing several narrow shavings (center photo, at left). Then cant the plane to the inside for several passes; then take a couple down the middle. Don't try to take a cut across the full width of the bevel until you make the last several passes (photo, bottom left). In a dense wood it uses a lot of energy to take a cut 1¾ in. wide, and I can now understand why in the old shops two people—one pushing, another pulling—were required to manage a large plane.

I have learned quite a bit from the experience of making these two planes, enough to realize that much lies ahead, for now I've got plans to make all of my planes for molding, rabbeting, jointing and other tasks. For those woodworkers who have never tried making planes, I would add that given a reasonable amount of technical reading, careful measuring and thoughtful joining, the plane's secrets unfold like the story in a good book. □

Robert Bourdeau is an accountant and an amateur woodworker in Laval, Quebec.

Restoring Bailey Planes
Wood-metal hybrids are worth the trouble

by George C. Gibbs

Photos: Barrie Svenson

Restored smooth plane has metal mechanism, wooden body.

In the late 1860s, Leonard Bailey began manufacturing wooden-soled planes with iron adjusting mechanisms. Stanley acquired the pattern, and these planes were sold in huge quantities until 1943. Cabinetmakers often preferred the resilience of wood to the harder iron soles of the newer planes, as I do. Many of these planes have survived, and I've found that they offer an excellent alternative to the rather tedious adjustment of all-wood planes and the impossible price of European wooden planes with metal screw mechanisms. Bailey planes frequently turn up in antique shops and at auctions and flea markets, although those in good, usable condition command high prices from collectors. But a great many more are in mediocre to deplorable condition and therefore quite reasonably priced. Since most of their problems lie in the beechwood block and not in the metal mechanism, they are quite easily made well again.

Before you buy the remains of a plane, examine its cast-iron body. If there are any cracks, reject it—they could be brazed, but the body is liable to warp. Next, make sure the plane is complete. The iron can be replaced if it is missing or rust-pitted, but the cap iron and lever cap must be intact. It helps if the knob and handle are in usable condition, but you can make replacements or salvage them from a plane that can't be repaired.

After you buy a suitable plane, begin with its wooden block. Some blocks require only a pass or two over the jointer to true up the face, although this has the undesirable side effect of opening the throat. Most will need more extensive surgery, either a new sole or complete replacement. Of the several ills that can befall a beechwood block, the most common is checking. Even small checks can render the cheeks of the block out of square, but all you need to do is joint the cheeks to square them up. Otherwise checking is no problem.

The screw holes in the block for attaching and aligning the frog mechanism are liable to be stripped. If the block is otherwise sound, you can drill them out, plug them and reset the screws. Or you can install a threaded metal insert in the block

and replace the old wood screws with machine screws. The accuracy and dependability of the plane rest largely on the ability of these screws to hold the frog tightly in place.

The least visible ailment is a warped or twisted block. Check it by placing the plane sole down on a truly flat surface, such as a saw table. If much twist is evident, it will be easiest to replace the entire block, since correcting twist will require flattening both the top and bottom surfaces.

Minor dings, dents and gouges in the cheeks and top of the block, while unsightly, don't affect the usability of the plane. But if an otherwise good block needs more than 1/16 in. removed to true up the face, a new sole is the best remedy. Take off all the metal parts and soak them in kerosene or mineral spirits to dissolve accumulated grime. Next, measure the block's thickness. This is critical because the repaired block must match the adjustment range available in the mechanism. Then joint or plane at least 1/4 in. of wood from the whole bottom of the block.

Any close-grained hardwood will serve for the new sole. Beech is best, but hard maple, cherry, birch, lignum vitae or rosewood will do very well. Prepare the stock about 1/16 in. thicker and wider than its finished size, but cut it exactly to length. The grain should run out toward the back of the plane, so it will polish itself in use. Glue the new sole to the bottom of the block with white or yellow glue and several clamps.

After the glue has cured, joint the new sole to the original thickness, being careful to maintain a true surface parallel to the top of the block. Then plane the sides of the half-sole flush with the original block, taking off a little extra if necessary to maintain squareness.

The next step is the most critical: cutting the mortise. The bevel and alignment at the rear of the mortise must be maintained, but this is easily done by guiding the flat side of a chisel against the remaining original bevel. To avoid splintering the new bottom when piercing, extend an accurate line from the rear of the mortise down one cheek at 45° to locate

Old plane (left) and old mechanism with a new block. Note the relief for the metal boss at base of frog.

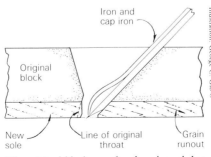

Original block

Iron and cap iron

New sole

Line of original throat

Grain runout

The original block can often be salvaged, but if the mouth is too large it will need a new sole. Orient the grain so it runs off the back, and keep the throat narrow.

Illustration: George C. Gibbs

To avoid splintering, transfer the mortise bevel to the sole, locate the mouth and chisel a narrow channel.

Planes and Chisels **41**

Beveled block guides chisel in chopping mortise in new beech block.

the rear edge of the opening on the sole. Then cut a ⅛-in. slot the width of the iron and about ⅛ in. deep into the bottom, just in front of the scribed line. Now continue to cut the mortise from the top, into the slot in the bottom. Keep the cut as narrow from front to back as possible; it will gradually be opened up later to fit the iron.

Finish cleaning the metal parts and reassemble the plane, carefully aligning the frog with the bevel at the rear of the mortise. Make sure the frog is tight. Try the iron with cap attached, and open up the throat of the mortise until it is barely large enough to allow the shavings to clear. Do not try to follow the original bevel at the front of the mortise, as the throats of most old planes are too large for fine cabinetwork.

Polish the cheeks and the bottom with very fine sandpaper and a flat sanding block, and lightly chamfer all the sharp edges. My favorite finish is a coat or two of tung-based penetrating sealer, followed by several coats of hard paste wax. Avoid building finishes such as shellac or varnish.

The amount of spit-and-polish applied to the metal parts is up to you, but for good results at least clean and lubricate with light oil all the moving parts and threads, and carefully grind and hone the iron.

Making a new block is somewhat more involved, although the procedure is similar. Beechwood is traditional, and it may be laminated if thick stock is not available. Avoid glue lines and edge grain on the bottom of the sole. The new block should be the same length and width as the original, but its length may be varied—it is perfectly possible to turn a jack plane into a jointer and vice versa, although a smoother is generally too small to convert. It will be necessary to clamp a guide block to the new block before cutting the mortise. Use 8/4 hardwood the width of the plane and long enough to keep the clamp out of the way, with an accurate 45° bevel on the business end. Use the remains of the original block to position it from front to back. Index the flat side of the chisel against the guide angle. If your chisels are too short to reach the bottom past the guide, go as far as you can to establish the bevel and then remove the guide. Again, be careful not to make the throat too large.

Before mounting the frog, chisel out a relief mortise for the boss at its front, and possibly a relief for the thumb screw as well. Use the original block for an indication, and from here proceed as described for a new sole. ☐

George C. Gibbs makes period furniture and once did it for a living. He is now drafting-room supervisor for a Denver firm that manufactures retail-store showcases and fixtures.

Q & A

Selecting tool steel—*It's time to retire my old Sears chisels and, I hope, move up in quality. I'm puzzled, however, by the flowery rhetoric I read in some mail-order tool catalogs. I've seen chisels made of high-tensile alloy steel, tungsten vanadium steel, chrome vanadium steel, high-carbon steel and even competition steel. Is there any real difference? I realize that if you buy cheap, you get cheap, but I don't know how to judge quality.*
—*Richard Fisher, Austin, Tex.*

JERRY GLASER REPLIES: It's impossible to make a rational decision about which tools to buy based just on the materials descriptions provided in the catalogs. Most hand tools are made out of plain high-carbon steel with precious little tungsten, vanadium, chrome or other metals added to alter their properties. The steels you mention get their names from alloying elements added to improve heat-treating properties. Names such as Sheffield or Swedish refer to the place where the steel is made, or serve as manufacturers' trade names to identify a particular alloy. Which steel is best for which tool? That's a question likely to provoke arguments among even experienced metallurgists. Steels for hand woodworking tools are selected as much for their suitability to mass production as for their ideal edge-holding properties.

For practical purposes, harder steels hold a keener edge longer, though the tradeoff for this durability is added sharpening difficulty. The most reliable measure of steels is the Rockwell C index, which ranks them by hardness on a scale from about 20 to about 70. Sight unseen (and untried), the Rockwell index is as good a way as any to judge the steel in a tool. Western chisels, gouges and plane irons are likely to be in the high 50s on the Rockwell C scale, while Japanese edge tools, with laminated steel edges, will be in the 60s. Turning tools will usually rank in the 50s unless they are made of high-speed steel, in which case they may be 60 or harder.

Absent any other way of judging tool steels, I'd suggest asking the manufacturers of the tools you have in mind for the Rockwell numbers of their products. You can then buy a couple made of the hardest steel and try them out. If they do the job and work better than the ones you had before, you have a winner. Keep in mind, however, that steels from a particular manufacturer aren't always consistent from tool to tool; variations of a few points either way are common. And steel hardness needn't be the sole criterion by which to evaluate a tool. Your sharpening skills, the woods you like to work, even the shapes and styles of handles will all bear on your success, and could easily offset a few points difference on the Rockwell scale.

Saving a blued chisel—*The factory bevel on my woodcarving tools was too blunt, so I ground them to a more suitable bevel on my bench grinder. Despite my best efforts to avoid overheating, about ¼ in. of the edge discolored, presumably ruining the temper. Is it okay to just grind away the discolored metal and proceed with honing? Or would it be better to try to retemper the blade?*
—*Roderick Shaw Jr., Tampa, Fla.*

JERRY GLASER REPLIES: Losing the temper of a tool to the grinding wheel is a common problem and one I've experienced many times myself. The simplest solution is to grind away the blued portion and start over. Only the heat-affected zone is softened, and by removing the blue, you'll be getting back to the tempered part of the tool. I don't advise retempering by heat-treating. Manufacturers have a difficult enough time producing tool steels of consistent hardness, and attempting it at the home-shop level is liable to be disappointing. Some machine shops do heat-treating, but the process is expensive and doubtful since the exact composition of the steel must be known in order to temper it correctly.

Grinders burn tools for several reasons, but the small wheels most home-shop grinders have, coupled with too vigorous metal removal, are frequently to blame. Using a small wheel, say, 6-in., makes it easy to grind the tool at an included angle that is too small. The resultant edge is thin and can't conduct the heat of grinding into the tool body fast enough to prevent bluing. If the wheel is a fine-grit, the problem is worse because the wheel cuts more slowly, tempting you to push harder. I find that an 8-in. dia., 1-in. wide, aluminum oxide wheel, such as a Norton 32A60-J5VBE or its equivalent, is suitable for most tool grinding. This is a 60-grit, medium-hardness wheel designed specifically for fast, cool cutting of tool steel. A clogged wheel invariably burns tools. So before any grinding job, I suggest you resurface and true the wheel with a grinding wheel dresser, a tool available from industrial supply houses.

If you use a light, consistent touch and don't grind the edge at too shallow an included angle, you should be able to remove the softened steel without further bluing.

Setting the hoops on Japanese chisels—*I recently bought a set of Japanese chisels and find they work quite well—with one exception. About every third time I hit one with my mallet, the metal hoop on the top of the handle goes flying off. What am I doing wrong?* —W.B. Lord, New York
TOSHIO ODATE REPLIES: Japanese chisel handles are tapered with a steel hoop at each end. The lower hoop works like a socket and is tightly fitted at the factory. The upper hoop has a larger opening at one end and goes on the handle first. The old Japanese name for this hoop is *sagariwa,* meaning "coming down ring." When this hoop slides down, it tightens around the handle and keeps it from splitting. On new chisels, the upper hoop usually fits loosely, and its inside edges are rough and burred. This is not good for sliding down, so with a round file make the inside of the hoop smooth and slightly convex, as shown. Do not file too much; try to keep the hoop fitting tightly. It should seat about ¹⁄₁₆ in. below the top of the handle. Then dip the tip of the handle in water for a few seconds and use a hammer to mushroom the wood over the hoop.

The lower hoop of the chisel usually is correctly fitted, but sometimes you must adjust it. There should be ¹⁄₁₆ in. clearance between the top edge of the hoop and the handle to stop the socket from digging into the wood and splitting it. Cut this space on your chisels if it is too small.

Mushroom handle over ring.

Use a round file to smooth and shape inside of hoop slightly convex.

Cut this space with a chisel if necessary.

Fire-hardened tool handles—*Will you please give me a few pointers on how to fire-harden the hickory tool handles I make?* —William Hood, Ebberton, Ga.
DREW LANGSNER REPLIES: Some years ago, the USDA Forest Products Laboratory ran tests on fire-hardened tool handles. The results demonstrated that this practice doesn't improve strength or durability. The FPL concluded that fire-hardening is purely cosmetic—a gimmick to sell tool handles.

I don't fire-harden handles anymore, but until I learned better, I fire-hardened tool handles with a propane torch by simply scorching the wood surface for the desired effect.

Backs not flat—*I recently purchased a set of heavy-duty socket firmer chisels. I am bothered that the chisel blades, all of them, have been ground on the flat side. That is to say, the back of the blade is not perfectly flat—each has a 4° or 5° bevel toward the front of the blade. The front edge is ground correctly—at about 30°—if you don't count the 5° bevel on the flat. Is this normal and correct?*
—Fred Silva, Santiago, Chile
This is not correct, but it is normal. Some factories finish such tools on belt sanders, which unavoidably dub over what ought to be a flat surface. You can correct the condition by lapping the back of the chisels on a coarse oilstone, or on carborundum cloth taped to a flat surface such as a saw table. Use plenty of oil.

How grind mortise chisels?—*I read an article in a British journal where a cabinetmaker states that a hollow grind on a mortise chisel is wrong and renders it useless. He claims that a correctly sharpened mortise chisel has a convex profile. Could you comment?*
—Barry Schwartzberg, Forest Hills, N.Y.
The profile of a mortise chisel can be convex, concave or straight. In any case, the angle of grinding can vary considerably, and this is of as much consequence as the profile. The grinding angle and profile, like so many decisions in working wood, will depend on the wood that's being cut, its density and the amount of waste to be removed. With a convex profile, the blade will be pushed away from the tissue. In cutting

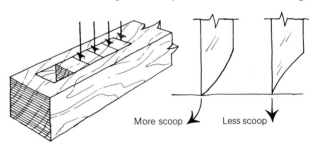

More scoop   Less scoop

large joints, such as those used in timber framing, there is a place for this profile. Likewise, if you want to take large bites out of the mortise with each move, then the scooping action will be assisted by the convex profile. Under either of these conditions, a hollow-ground blade is liable to break or would be less effective in its scooping action.

Now consider a ¼-in. wide, through mortise in a piece of cherry that's ½ in. thick. The hollow-ground chisel would be perfectly good for this. The chisel with the convex profile would be clumsy. In either case, a straight-ground chisel would perform well. —Ian J. Kirby

If the grind is too hollow, the chisel tip may break off.

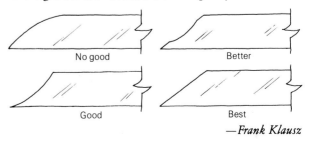

No good   Better

Good   Best

—*Frank Klausz*

Vietnamese Planes
Cong Huy Vo turns scrap into tools

by Curtis Erpelding

Grasping his homemade jack plane by the handles set behind its blade, Cong planes an edge. He controls the cut with his wrists, index fingers and thumbs.

When Cong Huy Vo, a Vietnamese boat refugee and furniture maker, settled in Portland, Oregon, he quickly found a job in a small antique shop. The first day at work, after looking around in dismay at the shop's limited selection of tools, he immediately set about making his own. I was beginning to make tools myself, so on a friend's recommendation, I paid Cong a visit.

Passing through the showroom full of Mission Oak and Grand Rapids-style pieces from the turn of this century—considered antiques here in the West—I entered the workshop in the rear of the store. Cong, a short, wiry man looking a decade younger than his 35 years, greeted me with a shy smile. He speaks only a few words of English, but with the traveler's repertoire of facial expressions and pantomime we communicated. He told me about his life in Saigon, his apprenticeship and his tool making.

When he was 14 years old, Cong apprenticed with his great-uncle, working four years for only room and board to learn the skills of carver and cabinetmaker. The apprentices all learned to make their own planes and carving tools, since there were few manufactured tools and little money to buy them. This necessity was no disadvantage. As Western woodworkers are rediscovering, home-made tools aren't that difficult to make, and they can be designed and modified to suit the individual and the problem at hand.

About 20 people, two per bench, worked in the Saigon shop. Apprentices learned how to work by hand, even though the shop had basic stationary machines: table saws, jointers, and so on. Each apprentice made a piece of furniture from start to finish, from the framing-out and carcase work to the carving, detailing and finishing. At the end of his apprenticeship Cong, like every other graduate, was dismissed—cheap beginners were preferred to wage-earning journeymen. Cong quickly set up his own workshop, training his brother, father and uncle to make everyday furniture and, from time to time, an elaborately carved cabinet for a wealthy client. In 1979, Cong left Vietnam, crammed with 33 others in a boat only 33 feet long, 8 feet wide and 3 feet deep. After 15 days at sea and 8 months in Thailand, Cong arrived in Portland. He brought nothing with him but his skill.

I first met Cong about six months after his arrival. He'd already made a bench plane as long as the western jack (about 14 in.), a rabbet plane, a dovetail plane with metal sole, and several special molding planes. Each had a simple beauty and logic, and some had features that were new to me. All the planes were made of a dense tropical hardwood resembling wengé, provided by the owner of the shop.

To make a plane, Cong dresses a block of wood to the appropriate size, then scribes lines for the opening with a square and his simple marking gauge. He bores out the waste and chisels the opening for the iron: mouth, throat and bed. The inner surfaces looked reasonably clean to me, but Cong pointed to the bed where the iron would rest and shook his head disapprovingly. It needed further smoothing, which Cong accomplished with a float, a file-like tool traditionally used for this purpose by makers of wooden planes (see page 46). Cong made his float by heating an old file to red hot and cooling it very slowly. The steel thus annealed, Cong easily filed or ground off the old teeth and cut new, deep ones with a cold chisel, straight across the file, spaced about ⅛ in. apart. He hardened the float by reheating it to a red color and then quenching it in oil.

Cong cut his jack-plane iron and cap iron from a used industrial hacksaw blade. The wedge, a piece of drill rod bent

A quick marking gauge

Cong's marking gauge consists of two ½-in. dowels and a wooden block, and can be made in a few minutes. Bore a ½-in. hole for the beam through the center of the block. With a ⁷⁄₁₆-in. machine bit, bore a hole for the wedge at a right angle to the beam hole, just breaking through its side wall. Taper the wedge hole by moving the drill bit around in it. You can avoid widening the bottom of the hole by clamping a piece of scrap to the gauge block, slightly wider than the gauge block and bored with a hole of the same diameter. The center of rotation will be in the scrap, ensuring a straight taper through the gauge. Carve or sand the dowel to fit snugly and drive a small brad through the end of the beam. You can make several gauges at once: substitute a pencil lead or a slitting cutter for the brad, or make longer beams for panel marking.

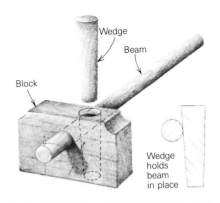

Wedge

Beam

Block

Wedge holds beam in place

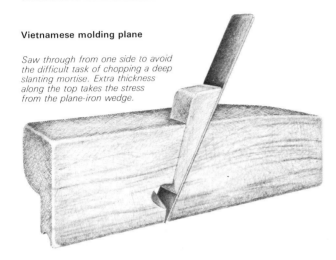

Vietnamese molding plane

Saw through from one side to avoid the difficult task of chopping a deep slanting mortise. Extra thickness along the top takes the stress from the plane-iron wedge.

to a U-shape with its ends tapered, is held in place by a pin that spans the plane's throat. The plane is adjusted with a steel hammer, as are Japanese planes. Their construction also resembles that of Japanese planes, but Cong pushes instead of pulls all of his planes. A ½-in. dowel fixed through the block behind the iron and wedge serves as a handle. The old floor-jack and crown-molding planes of the West also had dowel handles. Fixed through the plane's nose, the handles were pulled by an apprentice while the plane was guided by a journeyman. Cong's are one-man planes. He planes by grasping the dowel with one or both hands, standing beside a long board or behind a short one. He does not take a long, continuous shaving, but planes one area at a time as he moves down the board.

Because of their wide throats and poor-quality-steel irons, none of Cong's planes cut as cleanly, as free from tear-out or plane marks, as Japanese or Western wooden planes. In Vietnam, Cong's ordinary furniture didn't require highly finished flat surfaces, and the frame-and-panel construction of his ornate pieces was carved and embellished with split turnings. Planes were used to rough out the framework and panels, and to cut moldings. When flat, unblemished surfaces were required, they were scraped.

Several of Cong's molding planes feature an unusual and simple construction. By cutting the mouth and throat opening for the iron and wedge through one side, he avoids the tedious task of cleaning out an angled, closed mortise. After marking the opening on the face, Cong saws down as deep as

the width of the cutting iron, then chisels out the waste. The thick upper part of the plane accommodates the stress from the wedge, and only the bottom inch or so of the sole is as narrow as the iron, which can be the same width throughout its length. As there is no need for a narrow offset tang like on Western molding plane irons, the wedge can cover the entire width of the iron, reducing chatter. The bodies of some of his edge-molding planes extend below the plane iron, and serve as fences that guide the cut. Like Western planes, the 55° to 60° pitch of the irons in Cong's molding planes is steeper than the 45° pitch of his jack and rabbet planes. This steeper pitch produces more of a scraping cut, reducing tear-out, an important feature since the plane has no cap iron.

Living up to the Vietnamese reputation for resourcefulness, Cong has scavenged many of the materials he uses in his tools. He has ground scratch blades and scrapers from hacksaw blades and from straps of spring steel salvaged from the guts of an overstuffed chair. His gouges are made from lengths of drill rod, using a forge, electric blower and anvil given to him by a neighbor. He shapes the gouges on a homemade swage block made by boring various diameter holes through a chunk of iron and then hacksawing through these at an angle to produce shallow, tapered hollows.

Cong hammers the heated drill rod between a groove in the block and a bar slightly smaller than the groove's diameter. After the general sweep of the gouge has been forged, he grinds the back and edge profile, files or grinds the bevel and tapers the shank to form a tang. The gouge is hardened by reheating to cherry red followed by a quenching in oil. As far as I could tell, Cong did not temper any of his tools after he had hardened them. I watched him make a gouge from the forging to the handle-fitting in 15 minutes, so if one breaks or cracks, another can be made on the spot to take its place. Cong's tools may be rough and ready, but he knows how to get the most out of them.

I visited Cong again last fall. He has married, acquired two cars and moved into a nice apartment. He is still repairing and restoring old factory-made furniture. But he would like to have the chance to make the kind of furniture he made in Vietnam. His tools are evidence of his skill, skill that continues a tradition of self-reliant technology in woodworking. ☐

Curtis Erpelding makes furniture in Seattle, Wash. He has taught planemaking in a number of workshops around the country. Photo by the author.

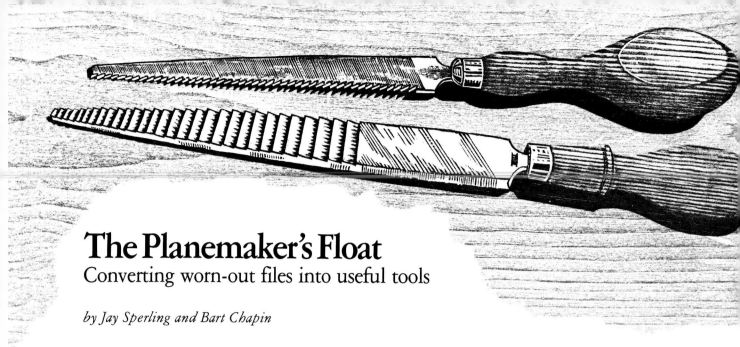

The Planemaker's Float
Converting worn-out files into useful tools

by Jay Sperling and Bart Chapin

Floats are toothed, file-like tools used in making wooden planes. They were widely used when cabinetmakers built their own planes, but now this versatile tool has been almost forgotten. A float cuts faster than a file and cleaner than a rasp. It's particularly adept at removing wood from hard-to-reach spots. Though chiefly used for wooden planes, it can do various jobs requiring controlled stock removal.

Traditionally made in a variety of shapes, floats are of two basic types: edge floats and flat-sided floats. Edge floats are fairly narrow in section and have teeth on their edges. They look like fat sawblades, and can cut narrow grooves and slots in tight quarters. The planemaker would saw each side of the wedge slot and then remove the waste between the two kerfs with the flat float, which he could also use to trim the walls to fit the wedge.

Unhardened, a float is quite easy to sharpen, and one sharpening is usually sufficient for making one plane. We'll give directions for making the flat-sided float, since it's more useful than the edge float. You can make the edge float following the same methods.

Make the blank from a worn-out flat file. You will have to soften (anneal) it by heating it red-hot with a torch and letting it cool gradually. If the file overheats and sags, pound it flat.

Next, grind off the file teeth. Select one side for the new teeth and take care to keep it perfectly flat. Remove any ripples with a flat mill file. Most planemakers didn't taper the thickness of floats, but a tapered tool is easier to use in tight places. Grind away enough

metal to form a gentle taper toward the tip. The float must be stiff along its entire length, so don't taper it too thin. (Edge floats must have a uniform thickness.) Beware of hard spots in the steel.

Flat-sided floats taper in plan pretty sharply toward their tips. A typical float 7 in. to 10 in. long and ¾ in. wide should taper to ⅛ in. at the tip. Edge floats taper in elevation from about ½ in. to ¼ in. at the tip. You can adjust these dimensions to suit the use of the tool. When grinding down the sides of the blank, keep the edges smooth and equal on both sides. Then fair the edges with a mill file and emery paper so they won't scratch your work. The edge float has a straight cutting edge. Grind and file it flat, referring to a straightedge regularly.

Although the teeth on traditional floats are uniformly spaced, I prefer to graduate the distances between teeth; this helps to make the tool cut more smoothly and eliminates chatter. At the tip of the tool the teeth are a little less than ⅛ in. apart; this distance increases in approximately 0.005-in. increments until the teeth at the back are close to ¼ in. apart. This allows a fine starting cut and greater stock removal afterward. Laying out the teeth for the first time, you should use a rule to graduate the distance between the teeth. Using a carbide-tipped scriber, etch in the lines at right angles to the centerline of the blank. Do this by clamping the blank near the edge of a worktable (centerline parallel with the

edge) and striking off the lines with a square. Flat-sided floats are toothed for only about two-thirds of their length, while edge floats are toothed along their entire length.

To cut the teeth you will need a pair (one large, one small) of triangular files and a file card. The file card is essential as the files can clog quickly. Clamp the blank down, and beginning at the tip and working back, thicken the scribed line with a couple of strokes of the file (step 1). Then, using the larger file on all but the smallest teeth, deepen the V-groove, while forming the relief angle on the back of the previous tooth. Stop filing the gullet when the file just nicks the top of the previous tooth (step 2). If you cut further, your teeth will not be level. With your last few strokes, push the cutting corner of the file toward the back, beginning the process of forming the tooth behind. As you work up the blank and the spacing increases, cuts will become deeper and wider. Don't overcut. You can always go back and correct the tooth shapes. When done, check the level of the teeth with a straightedge.

Now take your smaller triangular file and finish filing the teeth to get a 0° rake angle on each (step 3). Continue filing until the teeth are sharp. Recheck the teeth for uniform height a last time, and you're ready to fit the handle to the tang. To resharpen, repeat the process of filing the teeth backs with the large file and filing the face of the teeth with the small one. □

Jay Sperling is a freelance writer and Bart Chapin is a cabinetmaker. Both live in Bath, Maine.

STEP 1 STEP 2 STEP 3

Woodcuts: E. Marino III

Chisels, and How to Pare
Master the grip and stance before tackling joinery

by Ian J. Kirby

The first step in learning to work wood by hand is mastering the three basic cutting tools: the chisel, the plane and the saw. Each tool requires its own hand grip and body stance for the most effective transmission of power to the cutting edge. The best way to acquire skill is to practice using each tool until the proper techniques become second nature. In this article, I'll illustrate these concepts by showing how to use woodworking chisels.

I cannot overemphasize the importance of practicing fundamental tool skills before you attempt to make joints, let alone whole pieces of furniture. I constantly find beginning woodworkers who are struggling to learn some vital technique in the course of making furniture, with no attempt to develop and perfect their skills before the main event. The result will at best be a nondescript article of furniture that prominently features the scars of its maker's struggle, and at worst it will be failure and disillusionment. Either way, it seems futile. On the other hand, once you have learned how to use the tools, making joints is a simple procedural application of those skills; making furniture is, in large part, the application of jointmaking skills. No manipulative skill is acquired without practice. The potter, the dentist, the athlete—indeed, anyone wanting motor skills—must practice, and practice hard. The woodworker is not exempt.

Fortunately, all of woodworking can be broken down neatly into a series of skill-development processes. In particular, total control of the chisel can and should be learned by diligently practicing horizontal and vertical paring, nothing else. Therefore the following photo essay first shows the techniques of horizontal paring, then vertical paring, and then shows the application of these techniques (plus sawing) to the through dovetail joint. I can only urge you to accept that it will be worth your while to practice with the chisel until you have mastered it before you spoil any good wood.

Central to becoming skilled with the chisel is learning the proper hand grip, and from that point on, going right through the body to the soles of the feet, learning the relationship of each part of the anatomy to the next part. After the grip, we must be concerned with the forearms and upper arms including the shoulders, next the trunk in relationship to the arms, then the pelvic girdle and legs, and finally the feet. To achieve just what's wanted at the cutting edge, the whole body must participate and be in accord. I find that most beginners are conscious of their relationship with the tool up to the shoulder, where their awareness seems to end.

Since there are two main ways of paring with the chisel, there are two different grips and stances to learn. Note that in either mode, both hands are kept behind the cutting edge. There are not too many universal rules in woodworking, but

Ian J. Kirby directs Kirby Studios, a school of woodworking and furniture design, in Cumming, Ga.

this has to be one of them: when using a chisel, power it with one hand, guide it with the other, and avoid a nasty cut by keeping both hands behind the cutting edge. It goes without saying that your chisels must be perfectly sharp.

Although many different chisels are available on the market, when you are deciding which to buy, there are only a few factors to consider. In terms of blade section, there are just two types: the square-edged or firmer chisel and the bevel-edged chisel. The firmer can do heavier work, and can even be pressed into service for mortising. The bevel-edged chisel (there is no standard blade thickness or bevel angle) can get into such tight places as pin sockets between dovetails and is most suitable for furniture-making.

There are three common blade lengths: patternmaker's (8 in. to 10 in.), bench (5 in. to 7 in.) and carpenter's or butt (3 in. to 4 in.). Patternmakers need a long chisel to reach into deep, awkward places. I prefer the long blade's feel and balance, and it seems easier to control. Patternmaker's chisels are nearly always bevel-edged, and are also made with a cranked handle for paring far out on a flat surface. The bench chisel is commonest amongst furniture-makers, whereas the butt chisel, a phenomenon of American mass manufacture, is the least useful.

For handles, the most prized commercial wood is boxwood; the usual alternatives are ash and beech. The handle is generally driven onto a tang that has been formed atop the metal

Woodworking chisels have evolved into a few basic types. From left, patternmaker's chisel, firmer, standard bevel-edged chisel with boxwood handle (the choice of many furniture-makers), socket bench chisel, Blue Chip, Japanese and butt.

blade, and seats against a bolster formed between tang and blade. Firmers, in order to withstand pounding, generally have a thick leather washer between bolster and handle, plus metal ferrules top and bottom. Paring chisels, which are not to be struck with a mallet, usually have a single ferrule (at the bottom of the handle) and no washer. A third style, called a socket chisel, in which a tapered cylinder turned onto the handle fits a conical socket in the end of the blade, can also absorb heavy pounding. Handles made of high-impact plastic are quite as good as wood. They are generally formed around the tang and have no ferrule. Even so, they can be driven with a mallet. Once there were numerous handle shapes, and chisels were named after them. Today manufacturers seem to have settled on relatively simple turned forms for both wood and plastic, although recently plastic handles have been injection-molded into new shapes as a result of research into effective grips for maximum control. The Marples Blue Chip, a rounded square in section, is one example.

The Japanese chisels now available generally follow the form of Western chisels, with one exception. The back of the blade is hollowed out, except at the cutting edge. This makes stoning the back of the blade a little easier.

When buying chisels, you get what you pay for. I'm inclined to stay with the well-known manufacturers because they use steel of appropriate and reliable quality. On a tight budget, I'd start with bevel-edged bench chisels in widths of ¼ in., ⅜ in. and ¾ in., filling out the set as need arises and finances permit. Since plastic handles are molded in place, they are usually in line with the blade from top and side views. This is not always so with wooden handles, so be sure to check. Also, examine the back face (flat side). Except for Japanese chisels, it should come ground absolutely flat, although it is often made convex by overly enthusiastic finishing at the foundry. Having to flatten the back can cost you hours of work at the sharpening stone. To avoid slicing the left-hand index finger, which guides the chisel, always take the sharp edges off the length of the blade. Place the chisel at 45° to its back on a medium stone and give it about ten light strokes. As with any tool, buy the best you can afford. One good chisel is better than two poor ones.

Horizontal paring

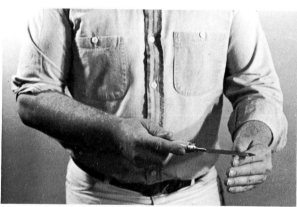

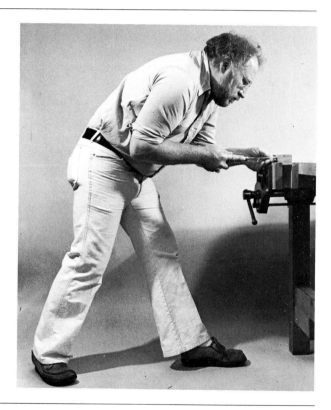

To pare horizontally, put the chisel in the palm of your right hand, index finger extended, photo above. (Kirby is right-handed; left-handers will have to reverse.) Line up blade, finger and forearm—this is the line that transmits the body's power. Rest the back of the chisel blade on your left forefinger, thumb on top, back of hand toward workpiece. This hand guides, and brakes, the cut. Now stand at the vise, take a step back with your right foot, and turn the foot so it's almost parallel to the bench edge, photo right. Bend at the waist and lock your right arm so your elbow is on or near your hip. Now push off with your right foot so the whole movement comes from your lower body and legs—your arms and trunk stay locked. You'll quickly find the most comfortable link of arms and body to suit your physique.

Horizontal paring is done on end grain when cleaning out dovetails (page 51, step 7), and on cross grain when cleaning dadoes and cross-laps. In either case, the wood fibers must first have been severed by sawcuts down to a gauge line. Then the waste comes out in stages, half from one side, half with the work turned around. The pattern of paring is the same, cross grain or end grain. To practice, mark out and saw a cross-lap housing in a length of 2x2 hardwood (lauan in the photo). Pare horizontally to just beyond the middle of the work, but tip the chisel alternately left and right so you reach the gauge line at either side of the housing while leaving a peak across the middle. The drawing at right shows this strategy of approaching the line in controlled stages.

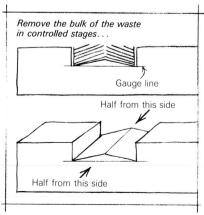

Remove the bulk of the waste in controlled stages...

Gauge line

Half from this side

Half from this side

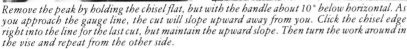

...and gradually approach the gauge line.

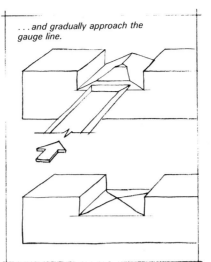

Remove the peak by holding the chisel flat, but with the handle about 10° below horizontal. As you approach the gauge line, the cut will slope upward away from you. Click the chisel edge right into the line for the last cut, but maintain the upward slope. Then turn the work around in the vise and repeat from the other side.

At this point the waste will be all gone, except for a small pitch in the middle of the housing. Remove it by raising the handle closer to horizontal with each cut, until on the final pass you feel the chisel go onto the gauge line on your side and see it exit on the gauge line at the far side. A little nibbling to clear out the corners, and you're done.

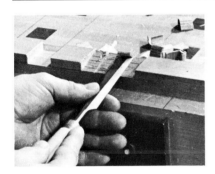

To cut a wide housing, saw the shoulders and saw a series of crosscuts spaced a little less than a chisel width apart. With the handle lower than horizontal, work a flat slope from one side and then the other, leaving a center pitch. Take small bites. The final cuts, as before, go from gauge line to gauge line. You'll find that this grip and stance provides ample power and control—the chisel should never come flying out of the wood on the far side. If it does, take smaller bites to get control of the relationship between the hardness of the wood, the sharpness of the tool, and your own strength.

Vertical paring

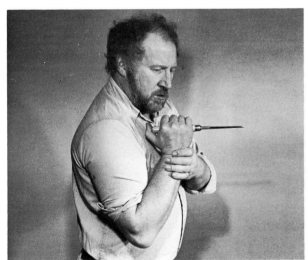

Vertical paring requires an entirely different grip and stance. Hold the chisel as if it were a dagger, thumb on the handle's end. Try to tuck your thumb into your shoulder joint. Rest the back of the chisel's blade on the middle part of your left index finger, left thumb on top of the blade. Stand with your left foot forward, and bend from the waist so the back of your left hand rests on the work. Lock your arms, rock your weight onto the forward foot, and flex your knees. All downward power comes from the hips and shoulders, not from moving your arms. Your head should move only as far downward as the chisel's edge moves, and no farther.

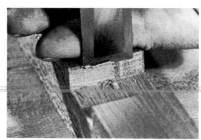

This grip enables you to concentrate the whole power of your body onto the cutting edge. The left hand, braced on the work, provides fine control and acts as a brake. Practice by paring the corner off a block of wood—you'll readily see, quickly learn to sense, any variation from the vertical.

Vertical paring is how we usually clean up tenon shoulders. You can practice on the walls of housings cut in the horizontal paring exercise. With a ¾-in. chisel, place about half the blade's width in the knife line and pare straight down. Move over half the chisel's width for each subsequent pass, using the knife line and the surface previously cut as your guides. Try to sense how every part of your body functions in relation to the tool, the workpiece and the bench. Practicing these basic techniques is worth all the effort you can muster, for confidence here will make joinery an automatic and simple procedure, not the tense and chancy event that discourages many beginners.

Chisel skills and the through dovetail

Paring with the bench chisel is one of the prerequisite skills for making through dovetails. The other major skill you will need for making these joints is sawing, which I'll review in the photo sequence that follows. Observe the stance shown at right; it's as important as any other aspect of the technique. I suggest that you practice dovetailing with hardwood stock about ⅝ in. thick and 4¼ in. wide. From the start, get into the habit of preparing the ends of the stock clean and square, by crosscutting with a carbide blade or else by knifing deeply around and hand-planing the end grain. When making drawers and casegoods, this end-grain surface provides the register that governs final fit.

It's possible to start the joint with either the tails or the pins, but I prefer to begin sawing the tails. This is because the tails are not cut straight down, but to an angle, and the saw is liable to wander. It doesn't matter whether the angles are constant, only that all the cuts are straight. If you make the pins first and transfer their angle to the tails, then you must cut a constant angle to a line—a constant angle not on the line won't do. If you have never practiced sawing down a line, draw a multitude of lines on scrap and just make cuts. It's worth emphasizing that the joint is made entirely from the saw. There's no need to chisel or file the side grain of the pins or tails. Although the joint has been elevated to a sort of ultimate standard, it's in reality simple—in no way

as difficult to make as the mortise and tenon. Don't be afraid of the dovetail.

Begin by gauging a line just less than the thickness of the stock at the ends of both pieces. After assembly, the outside surface of the stock will be planed to this thickness. Hold the wood upright in the vise. Using ¼-in. and ¾-in. incre-

ments, square lines across the end grain of the tails piece with a sharp pencil. I set the sliding bevel to a slope of one in six to mark the lines down what will be the outside of the joint (for practice, mark both sides). I carry these lines several inches below the gauge line to make it easier to sight the saw.

1. Sawing stance is not unlike that for horizontal paring. Three fingers grip the saw, with the index finger extended. With feet well apart, wrist locked, power comes from the shoulder and upper arm. The other hand guides the saw into the work. A good preparatory exercise is to grasp the saw, close your eyes, and attempt to set the teeth down on the bench—level and square. Open your eyes, check with a try square, and try again.

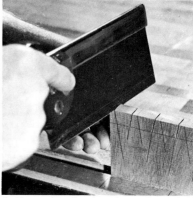

2. To saw the tails, place the wood upright in the vise. Square lines drawn right on the vise make this easy. Some people put the wood at an angle so they can saw straight down, but it's better in the long run to learn control. Start the cut with the saw at the tail angle, on the far edge of the wood. Spend the first strokes bringing the kerf across the end grain, then bring the sawteeth to level. Saw down the outside of the pencil line, leaving no wood between line and saw. Don't try to adjust the angle mid-way—you must have a straight cut. Do try to keep the sawteeth horizontal. When you are down to the gauge line at the front, you will also be down to the line you can't see at the back.

3. *Leave the wood upright in the vise and, standing as at left, remove the bulk of the waste with the coping saw. Its blade should slide easily into the kerf, down to within ⅛ in. of the gauge line. Rotate the saw's frame to twist the blade in the kerf, and it will turn the corner in its own thickness.*

4. *With practice, it's easy to keep the saw horizontal, and to cut very close to the gauge line, below. Some people chop all the waste out with a chisel. This is laborious, and some woods crumble so badly that the chisel pulls material out of the root of the joint.*

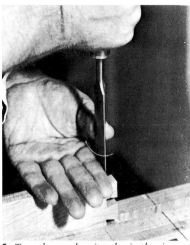

5. *Turn the wood on its edge in the vise and saw out the waste where the half-pins will fit. Clean up this shoulder by vertical paring, before turning the wood to do the other edge.*

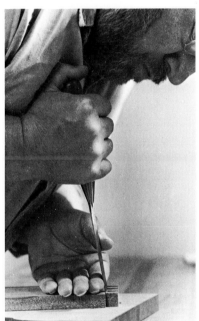

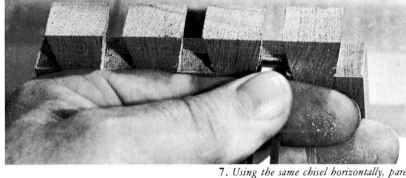

6. *To clean up the bottom of the joint, select the widest bevel-edged chisel that will fit between the tails and lay the wood flat on a cutting board. Pare down from both sides with the chisel about 10° back from 90° (left), until you can place the chisel into the gauge line. What's left is a small pitch in the middle of the joint. To remove it, place the wood upright in the vise.*

7. *Using the same chisel horizontally, pare straight across from gauge line to gauge line. The resulting surface will be flat and square, exactly where it should be. There is no virtue in undercutting the end grain, and no need to do so. Among other things, you lose the positive nature of the internal fit. Note that the initial incision made by the cutting gauge is where you finally place the chisel. An important part of the joint was completed at the start of marking out—a common condition in woodworking.*

8. *Now put the pins piece in the vise, projecting ⅛ in. above the bench top, and align the tails piece on it. You can adjust the fit of the joint according to the density of the wood by moving the tails piece minutely backward or forward. A tight joint in mahogany, which crushes easily, would be too tight in hard maple. Use a sharp knife to transfer the tail profiles, bearing down hard toward the outside corner. Then, with a square, pencil these lines several inches down the wood.*

9. *Saw the pins as you did the tails, endeavoring to split the knife line. If you fear the line, study what you are doing through a magnifying glass. You'll see that it's quite possible. A method of reminding yourself which side is the waste side is to leave the tails piece in position on the bench. Remove the waste with the coping saw, then pare the end-grain flat. Use the widest chisel that will fit the narrow side of the aperture, and sweep it askew to reach the whole surface.*

10. *Tap the joint home with a hammer, directing each blow to the center of each individual tail. You don't need a block of scrap to protect the wood, and you shouldn't substitute a mallet because it's liable to damage the work. On a wide joint, you'll hear a change in pitch as the hammer strikes a tight tail. This is the best way to isolate just which part of the joint needs adjustment.* □

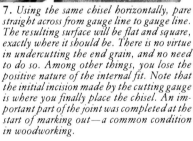

Planes and Chisels **51**

A Close Look
Micrographs illuminate sanding, scraping and planing

Photos by Stephen Smulski

The photomicrographs on these two pages show the surfaces left on hard maple *(Acer saccharum)* by various woodworking tools, along with the cutting edges of some of the tools themselves. The wood samples are all tangential surfaces from a plainsawn board, and the grain runs from lower left to upper right. The micrographs were made on Polaroid positive-negative film with an ETEC Autoscan scanning electron microscope. All but the last photo were taken at 50× magnification, although the first one, of planed wood, has been photographically enlarged to about 100×. For comparison we've reproduced at right the *B* from the word LIBERTY on the face of a Lincoln penny, also at 50×. The first and last photos are accompanied by further enlargements of the boxed portions of the *B*, at matching scales. To get the full impact of these photos, find yourself a penny before reading further.

Stephen Smulski was a graduate student in wood science when he took these photographs at the University of Massachusetts, Amherst.

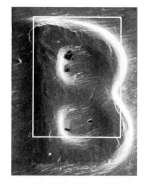

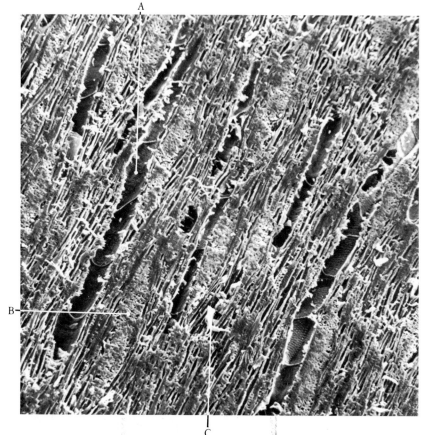

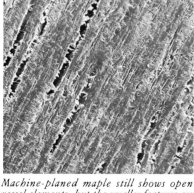

Machine-planed maple still shows open vessel elements, but the smaller features are obscured by torn and pounded fibers. The knife has moved across the surface from lower left to upper right, burnishing the fibers over onto one another. The jointer that did the work is routinely kept in good shape, and nothing special was done to it for this job.

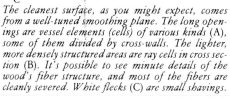

The cleanest surface, as you might expect, comes from a well-tuned smoothing plane. The long openings are vessel elements (cells) of various kinds (A), some of them divided by cross-walls. The lighter, more densely structured areas are ray cells in cross section (B). It's possible to see minute details of the wood's fiber structure, and most of the fibers are cleanly severed. White flecks (C) are small shavings.

The machined surface has been worked with a cabinet scraper. Most of the wood vessels are filled in by torn and rolled tissue, and the surface is scratched by the minute raggedness of the scraper's edge.

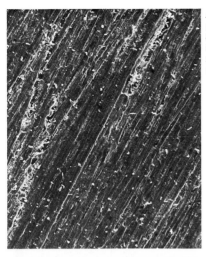

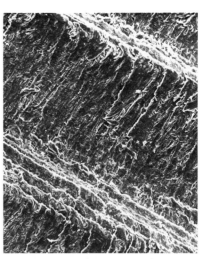

Maple hand-sanded with 220-grit sandpaper (Norton open-coat garnet) is just about as clean as the scraped surface, but there are more scratches. Dust (the white specks), rather than torn fibers, seems to have filled the vessel elements.

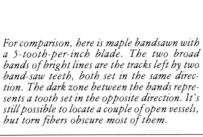

For comparison, here is maple bandsawn with a 5-tooth-per-inch blade. The two broad bands of bright lines are the tracks left by two band-saw teeth, both set in the same direction. The dark zone between the bands represents a tooth set in the opposite direction. It's still possible to locate a couple of open vessels, but torn fibers obscure most of them.

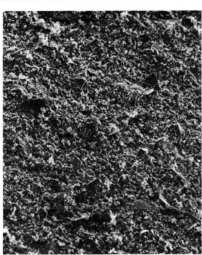

Sandpaper (Norton 220-A Openkote garnet finishing paper), new (far left) and after sanding the maple (left). What makes garnet good for sandpaper is its crystalline structure—the grit fractures into smaller, similarly angular particles. The used paper is littered with broken bits of garnet, maple dust and a few stringy wood fibers.

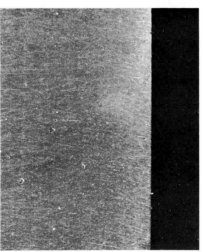

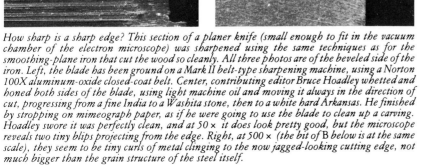

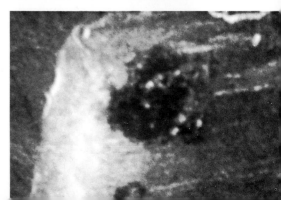

How sharp is a sharp edge? This section of a planer knife (small enough to fit in the vacuum chamber of the electron microscope) was sharpened using the same techniques as for the smoothing-plane iron that cut the wood so cleanly. All three photos are of the beveled side of the iron. Left, the blade has been ground on a Mark II belt-type sharpening machine, using a Norton 100X aluminum-oxide closed-coat belt. Center, contributing editor Bruce Hoadley whetted and honed both sides of the blade, using light machine oil and moving it always in the direction of cut, progressing from a fine India to a Washita stone, then to a white hard Arkansas. He finished by stropping on mimeograph paper, as if he were going to use the blade to clean up a carving. Hoadley swore it was perfectly clean, and at 50 × it does look pretty good, but the microscope reveals two tiny blips projecting from the edge. Right, at 500 × (the bit of B below is at the same scale), they seem to be tiny curls of metal clinging to the now jagged-looking cutting edge, not much bigger than the grain structure of the steel itself.

Using Bench Planes
These basic tools still do what machines can't

by Ian J. Kirby

In woodworking, there is no sound quite as delightful as the clear hiss of a sharp plane taking off a thin shaving. Nor can any other tool so precisely remove a modicum of wood tissue while leaving a perfectly flat and smooth surface. Of the three basic woodworking tools—saw, plane and chisel—the plane alone projects such a false sense of complexity that much modern woodworking is done without it. To be sure, many of its operations can now be done faster by machine. Where the cabinetmaker once had bench, plow and molding planes, he now has power jointer, router and spindle shaper.

For those woodworkers intent on a more developed level of workmanship, however, the hand plane still has an assured place in the shop. No machine, no matter how cleverly contrived, can match the plane's virtuosity in fitting drawers and doors, aligning twisted frame assemblies or leveling surfaces. The plane is unique in its ability to deliver a smooth, clear surface unattainable in any other manner.

Woodworkers of yesterday had dozens of planes to pick from. Though many are still available today, you need to own only one or two to perform most planing work.

In this article, I'll explain the various types and parts of modern metal planes, how to select and adjust them and, most important, how to use them. These principles apply to wooden planes also.

Why planes?—The woodworker's plane has been around for centuries. Unearthed tomb paintings depict Egyptian carpenters using planes to square up timbers. This remarkable history stems from the plane's basic usefulness; except for the adze and drawknife, no other primitive tool can prepare cleft or roughsawn wood to final dimensions. In its basic function and form, the plane has changed little: all planes consist of a blade or iron firmly mounted on a bed in the body of the tool. The blade must be adjustable and easily removable for sharpening. The bottom, or sole, of the plane must be kept flat and out of winding. The whole assembly, blade and body, must accommodate the hands or have handles so the operator can control the tool.

These requirements can be met with different designs and materials. Japanese planes, for example, are made of wood and are pulled. Western bench planes, whether metal or wood, are pushed. The result is the same: a smooth, accurate surface. Often the question is asked, which is better, metal or wood, and one can only reply that the answer lies with personal preference. Wooden planes are more difficult for the beginner to adjust and sharpen. A metal plane also delivers a clearer tactile sensation of the shaving being removed than does a wooden plane. Wooden planes can be made in the shop, and their soles can be flattened with another plane rather than with a grinding machine. A century ago, wooden planes evolved in such great variety because they suited the manufacturing technology then available. Each tradesman—

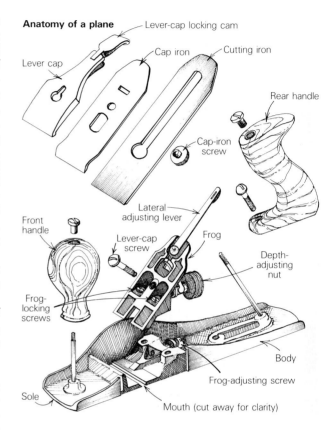

Anatomy of a plane — Lever-cap locking cam, Lever cap, Cap iron, Cutting iron, Rear handle, Cap-iron screw, Lateral adjusting lever, Front handle, Lever-cap screw, Frog, Depth-adjusting nut, Frog-locking screws, Body, Frog-adjusting screw, Sole, Mouth (cut away for clarity)

joiner, cabinetmaker, cooper, coachmaker, and so on—had his own array of planes suited to his own particular work. Some, an ogee molding plane for example, were designed for a single job and were thus used only occasionally. But the bench plane, because it could do many jobs well, was used constantly. The working specialty planes have vanished along with the trades to which they belonged, or else their functions are now better done with machines. The electric router, for instance, makes grooves much better and more quickly than plow planes can. Woodworkers today still need the utilitarian planing tools that the early tradesmen found so indispensable, and thus the bench plane has survived in very much its original configuration.

Three types of bench planes are commonly sold today, and these are distinguished by their lengths. The longest, about 22 in., is called a jointer. Of the lot, it is the most versatile; its length is designed for spanning and accurately flattening irregularities when making finished boards from roughsawn lumber. The smoothing plane is the shortest and has a body about 9 in. long. Its short sole cannot bridge irregularities in a board, so it's not the tool for making an accurately flat surface or edge. The smoothing plane is best for producing finished surfaces of high quality, when flatness is not impor-

Drawing: Rosalind Kirby

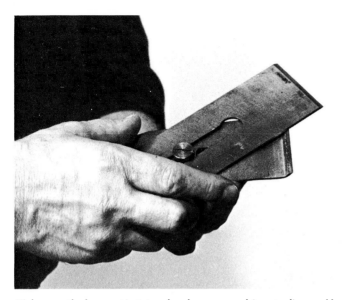

Kirby uses the lever cap's tapered end as a screwdriver to disassemble and assemble the cutting iron. If you use a screwdriver, make sure it is large enough to avoid damaging the screw. When reassembling, the cutting and cap irons should initially be put together at right angles, above left. The screw is then finger-tightened and the cap iron is rotated into place. The cap iron should be placed about $\frac{1}{16}$ in. from the back or non-beveled edge of the cutting iron, as shown below. For best performance, this distance is critical; if too small, shavings will jam and if too large, the iron may chatter. To put the cutting iron back in the plane, grasp the tool as shown in the photo, above right. Then, holding the cutting-iron assembly between the thumb and forefinger, drop it into the plane and make certain it seats against the bed and engages the depth-adjusting mechanism. At right, the frog-locking screws are loosened to move the frog forward and backward. Use your forefinger to feel how far the lower edge of the frog projects into the mouth.

tant. In the middle, at about 14 in. long, is the jack plane, supposedly named because its medium length makes it a "jack-of-all-trades." I've always found this plane to be of limited use—it has neither the jointer's accuracy nor the smoothing plane's handiness. If I were to buy but one plane, I would get the jointer. It will do its job as a preparation plane and can also be used for truing subassemblies and for finishing and smoothing work. I find little use for the jack except in instances where the jointer is uncomfortably heavy.

Adjusting the plane—Before it can be used, the plane must be tuned up or "fettled" (see box, page 57), its cutting iron must be sharpened and its various parts must be put in proper adjustment. Begin by removing the cutter and cap iron. With the plane on the bench, place your forefinger firmly on the lever cap and, using your thumb and middle finger, release the locking cam. Bear down with your forefinger to keep the lever cap from bouncing about. After you have removed the cutting-iron assembly, disassemble the cap iron from the cutting iron and sharpen the cutting iron (see the articles on sharpening on pages 63 to 87). Holding the cutting iron in the palm of your hand, loosen the screw just enough to slide the cap iron free.

After sharpening the iron, reassemble the cap and cutting iron, making sure the cap iron doesn't slide across or bump the sharpened edge. Tighten the screw and slide the cap iron to within $\frac{1}{16}$ in. of the cutting iron's edge. This setting is critical and getting it right may take some trying—too small, and shavings will jam; too large, and the iron will chatter.

To put the iron assembly back into the plane, grasp the body in the palm of your hand with fore and middle fingers at opposite ends of the mouth. Hold the assembly between your thumb and forefinger, and lower it into place onto your fingers. As the iron seats itself, you will feel it slide through the mouth to contact your fingers evenly on each side. Sight alongside the iron to make sure that it has firmly seated on the frog—the cast-iron assembly that beds the cutting iron in the plane body—and that the depth-adjusting mechanism has engaged the window in the cap iron. Place the lever cap over its screw and lock it down with the locking cam.

Adjusting the frog varies the space between the cutting edge and the front of the plane's mouth. This space should be made about $\frac{1}{32}$ in. if delicate shavings are to be made, although for hogging off roughsawn stock it might be $\frac{1}{16}$ in. or wider. The frog is held in place by recessed screws, and to get at them you'll have to remove the cutting-iron assembly

Grip the plane with your index finger extended (above). This triangulates the grip and gives you more control than wrapping all four fingers around the handle. When edge-planing, curl the fingers of your other hand up under the sole so your fingernails ride against the face of the board. Stand close enough to the work so that your shoulder is aligned with the cut (right). Standing too far away will cause you to tilt the plane, producing an out-of-square cut. Start the edge-planing cut with the toe held against the work (below left). Stand with one foot well below the work and the other spread about a walking pace back. The back leg should be straight, the front leg slightly bent (below center). Remember, this is a lower body action, not an arm movement. As you make the cut, uncurl your body and crouch into the work. Follow through by leaning well over the board (below right), extending your arms if you start to become unbalanced.

again. With the locking screws loose, a screw under the adjusting nut moves the frog forward and backward.

Unfortunately, the frog does not ride on a track; it can slew from side to side as it is moved. Its alignment can be gauged only with the cutter assembly in place, so the adjustment is a matter of trial and error. A likely starting place is with the leading edge of the frog just overlapping the mouth. Lock the cutting iron back in place, then turn the plane over. With the lateral adjusting lever centered, you want the cutting edge to be only $\frac{1}{32}$ in. from the front of the mouth. The edge should be parallel to the mouth opening. Adjust the frog to make it so, and recheck the adjustment with the cutting iron in place. When you've got it right, tighten the locking screws. Then apply a light film of machine oil to the frog, the cutting iron and the cap iron, and put the cutting-iron assembly back in place.

To adjust the cutting iron, back off the depth-adjusting nut until the cutting edge is inside the mouth. Then turn the plane over and sight down the sole. Turn the depth-adjusting nut clockwise until the edge of the iron appears as a black hairline projecting from the mouth. The edge of the iron

should be parallel to the surface of the sole; if it isn't, adjust it with the lateral adjusting lever. When setting the depth of cut, never adjust the plane to take a thick shaving with the intention of backing the iron off for a thinner cut. Start from zero and make small adjustments downward to get the shaving you want. Once you've got it, back the adjuster off in the counterclockwise direction until it just stops turning freely—this will take up the slack in the mechanism and keep the cutter from creeping downward and taking too large a cut. Smear paraffin or candle wax on the sole for lubrication, and you're ready to make a test shaving.

Select a board with an already planed edge, preferably not one done on a machine jointer. With the plane set for a fine cut, make a single pass and inspect the shaving. If it is uniformly thick and curls neatly against the cap iron, the plane is set correctly. If only crumbs appear in the mouth, advance the depth adjustment until a shaving can be made.

Using the plane—As with any tool, grip and stance are vital when using the plane. Other than working with a dull cutting iron, I find that ignoring these two points is the most common planing fault. Begin by learning to grip the plane: grasp the rear handle with three fingers and your thumb, and place the forefinger on the frog casting, almost touching the depth-adjusting nut. Resist the impulse to cram your forefinger around the handle. It will be uncomfortable and you will lose the triangulation afforded by the proper grip. For edge-planing, grasp the toe of the plane in your other hand, with your fingers curled up under the sole so your fingernails can ride lightly against the face of the board as a fence. If you are surface-planing, grip the plane's front knob in whatever manner seems most comfortable.

In learning stance, it's helpful to remember that planing is a push from the lower body, not an arm movement. Stand close enough to the work so that the shoulder pushing against the back handle of the plane is directly over the direction of the cut. Stand with your front foot well under the work and your leg bent; your rear foot should be spread about a walking pace back, and your leg should be kept straight or flexed slightly. As you push the plane over the wood, uncurl your body and crouch into the action.

Start the cut by placing the plane's toe firmly on the board. Maintain an even downward pressure on both handles as you follow through. Skewing the plane in relation to the direction of the cut will ease the work, but keep the entire length of the sole on the work. Boards to be edge-planed can be held on the bench in a vise, with dogs or against a bench stop. I prefer the stop because there is no chance of the work becoming distorted by undue holding pressure, and it forces you to learn to keep the plane flat against the edge. If you are doing it wrong, the board will just flop over. Boards to be surface-planed can be held against the stop, or else the continuous bench stop shown below can be made up of hardwood and clamped in the vise for wider support.

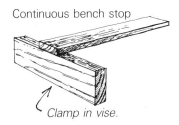

Continuous bench stop

Clamp in vise.

Contrary to the opinion that a block plane is the tool for planing end grain, I find that full-size bench planes are better for squaring and smoothing the ends of a board. All you need do is knife a line around the board to be squared and then plane down to the line, taking as light a cut as possible. To avoid tear-out, plane in from each edge toward the center, clamp blocks on the edge of the board, or plane a small chamfer on the edges.

All of the skills I've described in this article can be mastered with a perseverance that can be enjoyable. The plane is the ideal tool for many woodworking operations that are frequently done with power tools and sanders. Once you've tuned up and learned to control this tool, you will wonder how you ever got along without it. □

Ian J. Kirby directs Kirby Studios, a school of woodworking and furniture design, in Cumming, Ga.

How to tune up a plane

As a production item, the metal plane emerges from the factory as a nearly perfect tool. All the necessary parts are there, and made of materials suited to the job at hand. But if the plane is to be used to its maximum potential, it must be tuned up or "fettled." This means taking up where the factory left off by cleaning and adjusting the various parts. For a really superb job, enlist a machine shop to grind the plane's sole perfectly flat. Even planes with years of use behind them can benefit from this attention.

I begin fettling a plane by filing the cam that locks the lever cap and iron assembly to the frog. The cam works against a spring, and on new planes it is sometimes a bit rough and burred from casting. As a result it binds against the lever cap spring. Use a fine-cut file to dress the cam until it operates smoothly.

Next, true the end of the cap iron where it will bear against the cutting iron. It must rest perfectly flat against the cutting iron, or else shavings can jam up and break off in the mouth of the plane instead of curling smoothly away. You can do this on a bench stone. Keep the ground edge of the cap iron at right angles to its sides, so it will be parallel to the cutting iron's edge.

Use a straightedge to inspect the cutting iron for flatness in length and width. If the iron is bent along its length, straighten it by placing it over a block of softwood and bending it in the proper direction. Put the convex side up, and strike the iron sharply one or two times with a steel hammer. Final flatness is achieved by backing off on the sharpening stone. Next, tend to the brass adjusting nut. This nut should travel smoothly throughout. Usually, brass running on steel needs no lubrication. If you find, however, that a few drops of light machine oil won't correct a stiff nut on a new plane, send it back for replacement.

The most important, and difficult, part of fettling is getting the sole perfectly flat. I've tried several hand methods, with only marginal results. Now I send planes to a machine shop. The machinist makes up a cradle to hold the plane, so that a few passes of a precision grinder will flatten the sole. Leave the frog in place during grinding, or else the sole will be distorted when you torque the screws to reinstall it.

Planes come from the factory supposedly ground to tolerances of about 0.003 in., which seems quite fine by woodworking standards. Yet I've seen as much as $\frac{1}{32}$ in. of metal removed to achieve flatness. Grinding the sole is expensive and you have to decide whether it's worth the money. I find the difference quite noticeable; a well-fettled plane can take consistently finer cuts than one that has not been tuned. Before grinding, the edges at the heel and toe of the sole should be chamfered slightly with a file, to prevent burrs from forming if the tool is inadvertently struck against a hard surface. Lightly file off any burrs or paint on the inside of the mouth opening and on the working surfaces of the frog. Either of the handles can be shaped to improve comfort and grip: scoop out the rear handle near its base to fit your own hand. —I.J.K.

Preparation of Stock
The essential first step is obtaining a true face side

by Ian J. Kirby

A face side and a face edge are true reference surfaces from which accurate measurements may be taken. Proper preparation of a face side and from it a face edge are essential preparatory steps in woodworking. If this part of the job is not done correctly, one is bound to get into serious difficulties in all subsequent operations.

Preparing a face side that is flat in width, flat in length and out of winding is analogous to pegging out the site on which a house is to be built. If this first step is taken lightly and not accurately carried out, the errors compound at every building stage. No amount of connivance will prevent difficulties from arising at every turn. Yet of all the processes in woodworking, preparation of stock is often woefully done and frequently receives only perfunctory attention. Basic woodworking books do cover the process, and it seems strange to me that in teaching, the case for it must be constantly restated. I find that even quite experienced woodworkers need to be reminded of the procedures to follow. Preparation is so elementary that people seem to treat it with contempt, saving their energies for more interesting operations.

General approach

I shall discuss the general principles and requirements of preparation before going on to the specifics of obtaining true reference faces. It's always unwise to approach woodworking procedures in an ad-hoc manner because in the main there is a sequential logic to them. Preparation is no exception.

For any one job it is best to convert and prepare all of the stock at the same time, whenever it is possible to do so. This usually saves material, time and effort, and reduces the risk of making mistakes. It also ensures that all pieces to be finished to the same dimension are machined (if you are using machines) at the same setting.

Preparation includes or at least begins with the selection of timber for the job, if only because knowing what one has to achieve from a piece of wood has a lot to do with which piece one chooses. However, selection could be considered a topic in its own right and I won't try to deal with it here. Nonetheless, the two procedures overlap when deciding whether to cut all the pieces directly to the sizes specified in the cutting list, or whether to make it a multi-stage operation by preparing larger pieces from which the correct number of smaller pieces will later be taken. This depends very much upon the available stock, and it is worth spending some time deciding how best to proceed. For machining it's usually best to work with larger rather than smaller pieces of wood. Not only is time saved, but best use is made of the length of the machine bed. Thus one maximizes the possibility of achieving flatness, since flatness is, in part, a function of the length of the machine bed. On the other hand, the wood may be so long that it is difficult to handle, or the plank may be badly sprung, cupped or twisted. Machining out these defects will require many passes and waste a lot of material, and in such cases it pays to cut the plank into more manageable lengths first.

In preparing a piece of wood, whether it is a long plank which will be cut apart later or a single piece to be finished to a specific size, you have to assume that none of its six faces is an accurate reference surface. The first thing to do is to prepare a side which is flat in length, flat in width and out of winding.

The tools for testing these three characteristics are a long

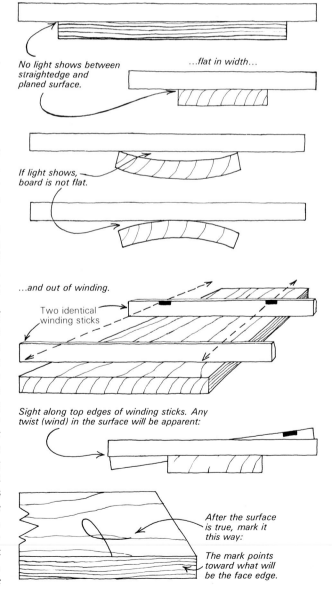

A face side is flat in length...

No light shows between straightedge and planed surface.

...flat in width...

If light shows, board is not flat.

...and out of winding.

Two identical winding sticks

Sight along top edges of winding sticks. Any twist (wind) in the surface will be apparent:

After the surface is true, mark it this way:

The mark points toward what will be the face edge.

straightedge and a pair of winding sticks. When a side of the board is flat and out of winding, it is marked and henceforth referred to as the *face side*. It is a reference surface from which further measurements are made. If it is not accurate, measurement can not be accurate.

Whether you choose to prepare one side in preference to the other on the basis of whether it will be exposed and visually important or for reasons connected to its role in construction is inconsequential to the primary fact that there has to be a face side. However, in many situations one does have to consider whether to put the face side on the inside or outside. The decision need not be too confusing. For instance, drawer parts should have their face sides inside, and the members of a carcase generally also have their face sides inside. This way, you retain an accurate reference surface no matter what you later do to the outside. Decide which side will be the face side by thinking ahead to the consequences of having this reference on the inside or on the outside. Since the outside surfaces of any job will be cleaned up by hand-planing or sanding, or perhaps by carving, the face side will be lost if it is the outside.

Do not, however, confuse the face side with the best-looking side. Frequently the two will be on opposite sides of the board. Also, the mark that is used to designate a face side is a clear statement that the side has been prepared and is flat in length, flat in width and out of winding. Never put a face mark on a board as a statement of intent. It is an after-the-fact mark.

The face side provides the reference surface from which a face edge can now be produced. The face edge bears the same three characteristics as the face side, plus a fourth: It is at 90° to the face side. All further measuring and marking can spring from these two reference surfaces, and most of the woodworker's marking-out tools are designed to rely on them. The marking gauge, for example, is used to mark lines on the wood parallel to either face side or face edge to indicate width and thickness. Because it gauges directly from these established reference surfaces, it is only as accurate as they are.

It is usual to mark and cut to width first, because less energy is involved in removing the material than if it were thicknessed first. Whether the board is planed to width or sawn first and then planed depends on the work involved. A good rule of thumb is that if there is enough wood to take a saw kerf and leave a small amount of falling board besides, then it is worth sawing first. If not, plane directly to the line. The same is true when cutting the board to thickness. Having now four of the six faces flat, out of winding and at 90° to each other, it remains only to cut to length.

Machining the face side

The machine used to produce the face side is the jointer or surface planer. It consists of two horizontal flat tables which are adjustable in height, separated by a revolving cutter block. The lead table (infeed) is in front of the cutter block, and the take-off table (outfeed) is behind it. The take-off table is accurately set so that its surface is perfectly tangential to the arc made by the rotating cutter. Thus when the wood passes over the cutter, it meets the take-off surface with no further deflection up or down. The table is set at this height when the blades are set in the cutter block, and it remains undisturbed thereafter. The lead table, on the other hand, de-

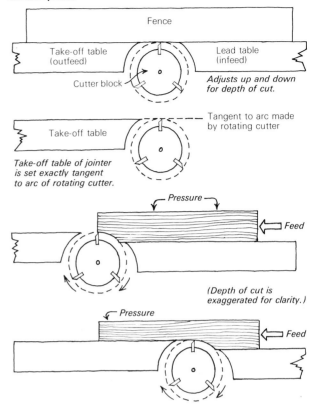

Surface planer

Fence

Take-off table (outfeed)   Lead table (infeed)

Cutter block   *Adjusts up and down for depth of cut.*

Take-off table   — Tangent to arc made by rotating cutter

Take-off table of jointer is set exactly tangent to arc of rotating cutter.

← Pressure →   ⇐ Feed

(Depth of cut is exaggerated for clarity.)

← Pressure   ⇐ Feed

termines the depth of cut and is constantly being adjusted for this purpose.

Mechanical feeds do exist but in the main the wood is offered to the machine by hand. It is held down firmly on the lead table and moved toward the cutter. At this point the wood has no reference surface, so the lead table is acting only as a carriage. Since the take-off table is set exactly tangential to the arc of the cutter, the cut surface will coincide with its surface. It is vitally important that this contact be established and maintained throughout the cut. Thus as soon as the leading edge of the wood passes the cutter, the operator shifts his hand to the take-off table and presses downward to maintain the contact, while no further downward pressure need be applied to the wood still on the lead table. Otherwise, the wood is liable to pivot or rock about the cutter and lift from the take-off table.

So long as the take-off table is set properly and the contact maintained between it and the newly cut surface, this surface will have all three properties of a face side, although it usually requires more than one pass to achieve. But provided the wood is not too badly sprung or twisted, two fairly light cuts will usually do. Two or three light cuts usually give a better result than one heavy cut, though the feed speed is of course also important in surface quality.

If the take-off table is set too low, the wood drops as it leaves the lead table and the cutters snip off the trailing edge of the board. If the take-off table is set too high, the wood tilts as it feeds and the cut is deeper at the leading edge, producing a taper.

Many shops lack a large jointer and attempt to achieve true reference surfaces with the thickness planer alone. But a thickness planer operates by pressing an already flat surface against its lower bed, to cut the top surface parallel to it. Its feed rollers apply enough pressure to straighten cup and warp out of a board. The board straightens as soon as it leaves the machine. Thus while it will produce a smooth surface, it cannot produce a flat surface unless the board is already flat on one side. It is better to hand-plane the face side and then thickness than to attempt to produce a face side with the thickness planer alone.

If I were faced with the financial problem of having to choose between buying a wider jointer or a thickness planer, I would probably prefer the jointer because you simply must be able to produce a true reference surface from a rough board. One solution, however, would be to use a European combination machine. These have one cutter block and two tables, a jointer on top and a thickness planer below. Wadkin makes several such machines, as do the Swiss Inca and Italian Combinato lines.

Hand-planing the face side

The long jointer plane is also known as a trying plane or sometimes as a fore plane, which probably comes from the word "before"—it is the tool used before anything else. There is a similarity between the jointer machine and the jointer plane in that both have a long, true surface. In both cases this long surface is the reason they are able to produce a flat surface on the wood. The trying plane is usually 22 in. long, enough for most work.

Also, while there is no difference in level between the toe and heel of the plane's sole, as there is between the lead and take-off tables of the machine, the toe and heel part do play a similar role to the machine tables. The toe and the surface in front of the plane iron act as the initial register, but the part behind the blade is most important in imparting flatness be-

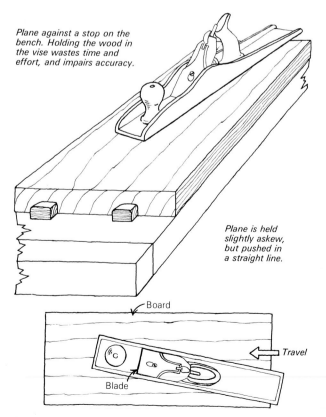

Plane against a stop on the bench. Holding the wood in the vise wastes time and effort, and impairs accuracy.

Plane is held slightly askew, but pushed in a straight line.

Board

Travel

Blade

cause it is guided by the improved surface of the wood. So it is vital to maintain pressure on the rear end of the plane to ensure contact and provide progressive flatness at each stroke. Since there is no difference between the two surfaces, the inherent tendency to lift from the surface of the wood is much less apparent than with the machine.

The piece of wood to be planed should, if it is of manageable proportions in terms of width and thickness and not too badly warped, be placed on the surface of the bench against a bench stop. A less good way to plane wood is to hold it in the vise. If there is a degree of spring or twist, the pressure of the vise will probably rectify it, thereby giving a false indication of the real state of the wood when being planed. On release the wood of course returns to its misaligned state. Apart from this, the time involved in mounting the work in the vise, releasing it and changing body position to do so each time the work is checked is much greater than the time it takes to lift the wood from the bench, check it and put it down again. Further, working against the bench stop obliges one to operate the plane properly and provides tactile feedback information that one would not get if the work were in the vise. For instance, if the thrust of the plane is not directly along the axis of the wood or is not being applied horizontally, the wood will react by either toppling over or skewing round on itself. Learners will avoid forming bad habits if they plane woods on the bench in this way. The assumption here, of course, is that the bench is accurate. The surface on which one planes must be horizontal. It must be a "face side" in itself and have all the properties of a face side. A piece of wood with much of one's weight being pressed on it through the plane will easily deflect a few thousandths of an inch. If the surface it is on is hollow, it will be planed hollow. A fine shaving is only about .0015 in. thick, and there is little room for error. When a lot of wood has to be removed, sharpen the plane and move its frog back to open the mouth and take deeper cuts with each pass.

A straightedge is used to check flatness in length and width. It is necessary to hold the wood and the straightedge up to the light to ensure that no light can be seen between the straightedge and the surface being tested. Don't despise checking the board by eye at any time without instruments. It would be foolish to claim that the eye can be developed to the point where measuring tools become redundant, but one should develop as keen an eye as possible—for one's own awareness if nothing else.

To check for winding, two accurately planed, equally dimensioned pieces of wood, known as winding sticks, are placed transversely at points along the length of the surface and sighted to read for parallelism throughout. The sticks need to be long enough to accentuate the degree of winding so it can easily be seen. The amount of twist can be gauged by the deflection of the sticks, and the remedy is to plane diagonally from the high corner at one end to the opposite high corner at the other end.

If the surface has interlocked or similarly awkward grain, set the plane mouth fine, the back iron close to the blade edge and keep the blade sharp, and it will be easy to plane diagonally or at right angles to the grain. Generally, the more dense the wood, the easier it is to plane across the grain. When the board is flat and out of winding, one should be able to take a clean, fine shaving from end to end all across the surface. When the surface is flat in length and width and

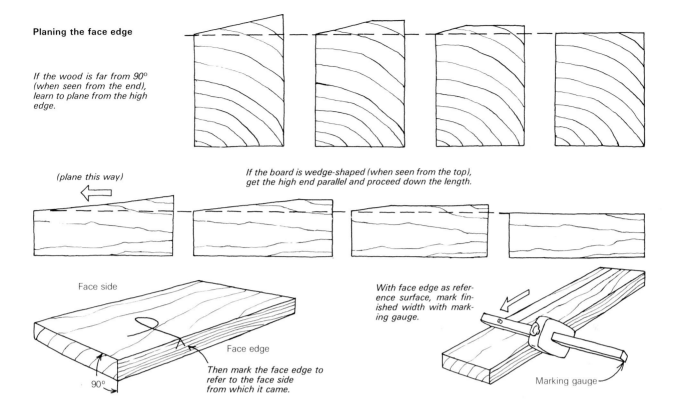

Planing the face edge

If the wood is far from 90° (when seen from the end), learn to plane from the high edge.

(plane this way)

If the board is wedge-shaped (when seen from the top), get the high end parallel and proceed down the length.

Face side

Face edge

Then mark the face edge to refer to the face side from which it came.

90°

With face edge as reference surface, mark finished width with marking gauge.

Marking gauge

out of winding, the face-side mark is applied to it in a position to indicate which edge will become the face edge.

The face edge

Machining the face edge on the jointer is like preparing the face sides. Pressure must be applied to the take-off table in the same way, but now the face side also has to be kept firmly in contact with the fence. The fence must make a 90° angle with the jointer bed, and it's worth checking with a square every time the machine is used. Both downward and sideways pressure need to be maintained throughout the cut, and the procedure is that much more difficult to control.

When preparing the face edge on the bench with the jointer plane, the wood should be stood on its edge against the stop, for all the same reasons as before. This will not be possible when the board is somewhat wider than it is thick, and there will be no alternative but to put it in the vise. But be aware of the problems of distortion that this might cause, although the difficulty is less than with a face side. If the wood is far from being parallel it might be best to thickness the piece before preparing the face edge.

If the wood is severely angled from 90° on its edge, one must learn to hold the plane with its sole horizontal and to take material from the high edge. Some find it a help to shift the plane sideways so the high edge of the wood is cut by the center of the plane iron, but on no account tilt the plane away from horizontal in an effort to compensate. If the piece is wedge-shaped in length, the usual procedure is to get the high end parallel to the face edge and progressively to achieve parallelism down the length of the board as the width—or thickness for that matter—is reached.

The checks for flatness are the same as before, but it is also necessary to check for right-angularity between the face side and the prepared edge all the way along its length. This is

done with a try square. When the four characteristics have all been achieved, the face edge is marked as the side was marked, this time in such a way as to indicate the face side from which it springs.

Width and thickness

The next thing is to use the face side and edge as reference surfaces from which to mark and cut to width and thickness, usually to width first. The first operation may be to saw, either with circular saw or handsaw, to within planing distance of the final dimension. One should aim to saw as near to the line as possible without touching it.

The subsequent planing by machine would be done with a thickness planer and is usually a one or two-pass operation requiring only that the thicknesser be set to the given dimension, the wood fed in and collected at the other end. It is important, however, to do all pieces that are to finish at that dimension at the one setting.

Just as it is not possible to produce a face side with a thickness planer, it is also impossible to plane to width or thickness on a jointer. The necessary accuracy comes from an already established reference surface, and the jointer is not designed to work from a reference surface. There is no guarantee that parallelism will result. There are commercial attachments for jointers to convert them to a form of thicknesser, but they have limited capacity and my inclination is away from them.

Getting to width and thickness by bench methods involves gauging all around with the marking gauge and planing to the line with the jointer plane. As before, work with the wood on the bench and not in the vise.

Length

Getting the material to length is a two-part process. One end is squared off first, either with a radial-arm saw, a traveling-

Sawing board

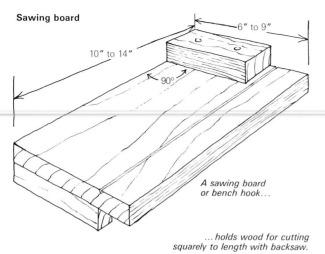

A sawing board or bench hook…

…holds wood for cutting squarely to length with backsaw.

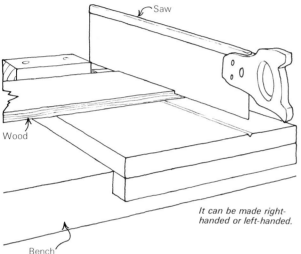

It can be made right-handed or left-handed.

bed dimension saw, or by hand. In the latter case the wood is quite deeply knifed all around, using a try square and working off the face side or face edge. Then saw with a backsaw, holding the work on a sawing board, or with a panel saw and sawhorses if it is a large piece. The length is then measured from this end face and marked with knife and square. The excess is cut in the same way as the other end, either from the marks made, or directly by use of stops on the machine saws.

If the prepared piece of wood is later cut into pieces, care should be taken to see that all the pieces bear the face-side and face-edge marks. For although rectangularity has been achieved, one continues to use only face side and face edge as the reference surfaces throughout all subsequent work.

Beginners are often confused about leaving extra wood for cleaning up. In general, one doesn't leave any extra. The cleaning-up process should remove very little material. It should be what it is called—simply cleaning. The same rule applies when cutting to length, except in the case of legs or stiles that are to have mortises very near their ends. To avoid splitting the wood, a ¾-in. horn is left on the end of the stock, to be sawn off afterward. That ¾ in. is a necessary piece, so cut to the finished length plus ¾ in.

End grain on square stock is difficult to plane, and the usual shortcut is to finish it on a disc sander. Probably the best way is with a shooting board, which controls the plane while supporting the end tissue of the wood. On wider stock it is relatively easy to put the wood upright in the vise, arrange some form of scrap-wood end support and plane as though working on the edge. The plane must be sharp, and a little paraffin wax helps greatly; the feel of end grain being cleanly cut is gratifying. □

Ian J. Kirby teaches in his own school, Kirby Studios, in Cumming, Ga.

Planing end grain

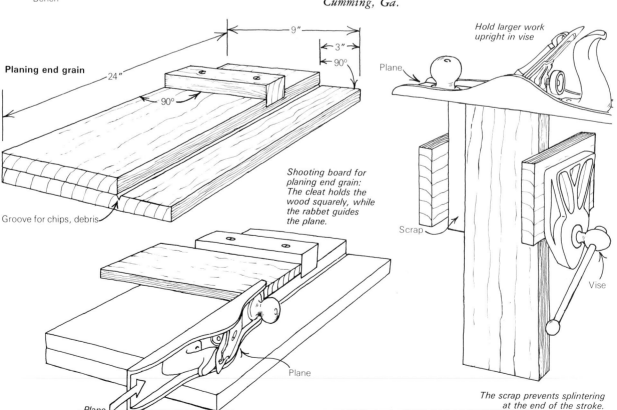

Shooting board for planing end grain: The cleat holds the wood squarely, while the rabbet guides the plane.

Groove for chips, debris

Plane

Plane

Hold larger work upright in vise

Plane

Scrap

Vise

The scrap prevents splintering at the end of the stroke.

Micro Bevels

'Dulling' the edge to make it better

by R. Bruce Hoadley

Sometimes the most basic and obvious principles escape our attention. A good example is microsharpening, a concept that can be used to advantage by every woodworker on a wide array of woodworking tools. The basic idea is simply to add a very narrow microbevel in the final sharpening, thereby producing a more durable edge.

When tools are sharpened, they are ground down to form a usually specified sharpness angle. The smaller the angle, the sharper the tool will be, but also the more fragile the edge and the quicker it will dull. Increasing this angle increases the durability of the edge but also increases the cutting force required to push the edge through the wood. The force may also be compounded by the clearance angle — the angle the bottom of the tool makes with the wood. With hand tools, the clearance angle can be virtually zero, but with power tools frictional heating requires a positive clearance angle. (With dull tools, the clearance angle actually becomes negative.)

So there is a trade-off involved — to decrease the cutting force required without decreasing the tool's sharpness angle to the point of making the edge too fragile. Adding a microbevel gives us a compromise. It increases the effective sharpness angle of the tool, but doesn't affect chip formation because the bevel is so narrow.

In carving chisels, as typified by the common gouge, a microbevel of about 0.005-inch on the concave face increases the effective sharpness angle to about 25-35 degrees (from 15 degrees) and will make a world of difference in longer edge wear. After the conventional sharpening is completed, the microbevel can be applied by light strokes of a round hard Arkansas pencil or round-edge slip on the concave face. This leaves the flatness of the clearance face undisturbed to ensure the edge will "bite" but modifies the sharpness angle. Determining the correct width of the microbevel may be aided at first by using a magnifying glass and hair for comparison. Eventually, the bright reflection of the microbevel can be gauged by eye, or the necessary number of strokes of the stone may become standardized.

The common bench-type hand plane can also be microsharpened to advantage. But to avoid interfering with chip formation, the microbevel should be added to the already ground bevel forming the under face. Keeping the microbevel to only about a 40-degree sharpness angle will ensure that a slight positive clearance angle still remains. This is the "honing angle" often recommended in plane sharpening.

With boring bits, microbevels can be added to the lips and to the inner edge of the spurs.

Instructions for sharpening planers, jointers and other machines having multiple-knife cutterheads usually recommend leaving a hairline of jointed surface on each knife. This jointed edge is in reality a microbevel.

Finally, a new jackknife, as it comes from the factory, usually has a "sharp" edge formed by double-bevel grinding which creates a negative clearance angle when held in the customary draw-grip position used in whittling. The knife merely rides along the wood surface without cutting. The blade must be reground to locate the edge along the lower face to give edge contact with the wood. Adding a microbevel on the face away from the work will improve edge life. □

Microbevel is bright vertical edge along greyish sharpened chisel face. Hair gives sense of scale. Arkansas pencil is used to put a microbevel on a gouge. Putting it on wrong side merely dulls the tool. Drawings show right way.

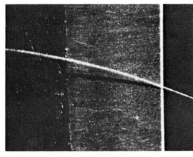

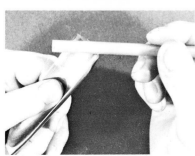

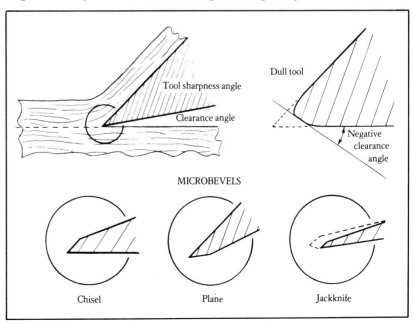

Whetstones
How novaculite is quarried and finished

by William G. Wing

Whetstones have been around a while, as the 600-year-old quotation from De Trevisa suggests. Stone tools were among the things that got people to come down from the trees and start acting like people. This isn't meant to suggest whetstones are quite that old, because stone cutting tools got their edges mostly by chipping and flaking. But even before metal tools were made, some edges were obtained by abrasion—by rubbing the edges on harder stones. When metal tools did come in, abrasion was absolutely necessary.

The constant problem in abrasives, though, is the trade-off between speed and smoothness. The brilliant insight that led to forming the abrasive in the shape of a wheel, the grindstone, gave speed but left a rough edge on the tool or weapon—all right for hacking off someone's head but not good for careful slicing. A "fine" edge could be produced only by final rubbing on something harder and smoother than the grindstone. This was the process that came to be know as whetting or honing. The fact that both words are among the few that have stayed alive and healthy from Old English shows how basic the operation is.

Workmen in every region had to find the best whetstones they could. When farmers pioneered into the wilderness of America, their survival depended on good cutting edges on axes and scythes. One can imagine them moving westward, testing any likely-looking rock on their axes. They picked up a lot of advice from the Indians who, as Stone Age people, knew a lot more about rocks than the newcomers did.

This is the way—by reports from Indians—that pioneers in central Arkansas learned of quarries producing superior white, almost translucent, spear and arrow points. There were Indian quarries in the Ouchita Mountains near the valley filled with hot springs (known today, appropriately, as Hot Springs). The rock was quarried in open pits, by fires built against outcrops, which were then cracked off by being doused with cold water. Some of the pits were so deep it was obvious that mining had been going on for a long time.

How quickly this hard rock was put to use as a whetstone is not recorded. It was early, though—a letter written in 1818 says that 200 pounds of whetstones, priced at $2 a pound, had been shipped out by flatboats on the Ouchita River the previous year. (The Ouchita runs into the Red River, which empties into the Mississippi.)

Hard Arkansas (pronounced "Ar-kan-zus") stones, and a softer variety that picked up the name Washita (from Ouchita), developed a market on the East Coast and in Europe but did not rise to the top quickly. A host of whetstone varieties were available in the last century: Ayr stone, snake stone, Charnley Forest stone, Norway ragstone, Cutler's greenstone, and so on. Remember that interest went

Bill Wing, of Englewood, N.J., is a writer and an amateur woodcarver.

far beyond the workshop—until the disposable razor blade was invented, every man had the choice of raising whiskers or learning how to keep an edge on a razor. Turkey stone, which was mined somewhere in Asia Minor, finished in Marseilles and shipped by the ton into America, set the standard of excellence. Eventually, though, it was superseded by Arkansas stones, of the mineral novaculite.

With such a background, with so many kinds of stones available, with a planet composed mostly of stone, why have Arkansas stones, from one little patch of hillside near Hot Springs, established themselves as the standard of excellence? To find out, I seized a chance to visit the leading manufacturer of Arkansas whetstones last summer.

The Hiram A. Smith Whetstone Co., Inc., is located on the fringe of the suburbs of Hot Springs. It is said to account for about 70% of the production of Arkansas whetstones, and it is now being run by the fourth generation of Smiths. James A. Smith, the president, is named after his great-grandfather, who got the family into the whetstone business because the land he had acquired for real-estate speculation happened to include the best of the stone deposits.

Until 1964, the company simply mined and shipped raw stone for finishing overseas. Smith's father, Hiram, began developing lapidary knowledge of his own. He developed a stone-cutting saw, essentially a flat steel disc about two feet in diameter. Small industrial diamonds—"sweepings"—were glued along the rims. The saw was mounted overhead, like a radial arm saw, but the operator pushed the stone through the saw while it was bathed with a stream of cooling and lubricating oil. In 1976, the Smiths built an integrated plant and now have about 75 employees and all the business they can handle. "I guess we sell about 100,000 stones a month," Smith said. Most are sold under other companies' labels.

Raw stones are found in the quarries within about 30 feet of the surface. Holes from four to eight feet deep are drilled in the rock with jackhammers, and then filled with explosives. Dynamite can't be used because it shatters the rock; instead, a low-density explosive, which goes "whoomp," is tamped into the 1¾-inch dia. holes. After the blast, every broken piece of rock is examined by an expert, who taps the rocks with a dressing hammer. More than two-thirds of the broken rocks are rejected and thrown on the waste pile. The rest, mostly in sizes slightly larger than the human head, are scooped up into a truck and carried a few miles to the plant.

The first process is cutting each piece of stone into its optimum size. The slabber has a sharp eye for chitchat (rubbish stone), quartz lines, sand deposits and short cracks, and he tosses away about half of the stone that has been brought in from the quarries as below standard. He then decides how to cut each of the remaining stones to obtain the longest possible pieces from each. The hope is to get 20-in. lengths, but novaculite is a much-fractured rock and such long pieces are rare. Next, dicers cut the slabs into standard widths, ranging from wide hones to pocket sharpeners. Then the stones are cut to standard lengths by clippers. The aim at each step is to produce a stone of the highest possible value.

After being cut, the stones are finished. From 200 to 300 stones are "lapped," or polished, at a time as they ride on a revolving iron plate covered with industrial grit. Polishing continues by lapping the stones with increasingly fine grits. Edge bevels are ground by hand on abrasive wheels. At the same time that these flat whetstones are cut and polished, files are cut and hand-finished in a variety of cross sections.

After finishing, the stones are assessed once more and about a fourth of them are discarded. The arithmetic doesn't quite work out, but Smith says that of all the rock quarried only about 5% gets to market. The surviving stones are then graded into four categories of hardness.

The softest and coarsest grade is called Washita, sometimes called calico stone in the old days because of its very showy grain and colors. This grade will produce an edge most quickly, but not an edge of the finest quality. The second grade up the scale of hardness is called soft Arkansas. This, a greyish and sometimes mottled stone, is described by Smith as the best general-purpose grade—that is, the best compromise between speed of sharpening and quality of edge. The next grade is hard Arkansas, a clear white stone said to be the best for the final polishing of an already sharp edge. Finally, at the top of the ladder, is black hard Arkansas, which Smith's catalog describes as the "supreme ultimate." Blacks, which range in color from ebony to dark grey, are for specialists, those who need to touch up an already extremely sharp edge. Because black novaculite is rare and hardly ever occurs in long pieces, its price is correspondingly high.

After grading, some stones are glued together in combinations of grades, some are glued on paddles or blocks and some are fitted into sets. The standard flat whetstone goes into a lacquered red-cedar box; the label under which it is to be sold is then stamped in gold on the cover. Smith no longer makes the boxes, but buys them under contract. (Smith has the best of both worlds with the red cedar. Its red and cream streaks make the boxes look exotic and expensive. Actually, the wood is readily available locally, since little cedar trees cover northern Arkansas and southern Missouri.)

Smith talks candidly about the fact that his company's control of its raw supplies and its insistence on selling only first-quality stones enable it to maintain fairly high prices. The chief reason for downgrading a stone from first to second-class quality is the presence in the novaculite of small pockets of a softer material, called sand pits. Seconds will sharpen an edge just as well as firsts, Smith says, unless the pits are so big they snag the blade. If you can find them, they cost only a quarter as much as firsts. But since quality is the essential reason for owning an Arkansas whetstone, and since they last so long that the initial price is amortized over a long period, there is little reason for buying anything except a first-class stone. Natural stones last longer than industrial ones, not because they are harder, but because the bonding agent that holds together the particles in manmade stone breaks down.

Insistence on quality also stems from the fact that Arkansas stones were hurt badly in the past when the market was flooded with bad stones. L. S. Griswold, a geologist who in 1890 wrote the only comprehensive work on Arkansas stones, told how inferior stones were passed off as first quality.

Blocks of novaculite blasted out of a quarry at the Hiram A. Smith Whetstone Co., Hot Springs, Ark. Only about 5% of the novaculite quarried will become finished whetstones.

Raw Washita stone has been halved on diamond-edged steel wheel.

Stones are lapped, or polished, on a grit-covered iron plate.

Often, they were polished with pumice because the powder filled and concealed defects. Smith says bad stones are still being sold; some of them are not novaculite at all but a softer mineral called tripoli.

How, then, can you judge a good stone in the marketplace? Smith said the customer's best procedure is to rely on the reputation of the company selling the stone. Also, he said, a good stone looks good. Griswold said almost the same thing in his book: "Good stones seldom have a poor finish." Check the edges and sides to see if they have been ground true. Griswold also recommends things that wouldn't be tolerated today: testing for defects with a knife point and scratching the surface with your fingernails. (If you can scratch it, the stone is soft; if your nails come off, it's hard.)

To use the stones, Smith advocates standard sharpening techniques. He is not a purist about lubricant: Use a little oil, he says, but if you don't have oil, use water. When customers complain the stones won't sharpen, invariably, Smith says, they are not using enough muscle. After use, he recommends washing the stone with soap and water, and then drying it.

Novaculite is a form of quartz, and it is almost pure silica. Technically, novaculite is a kind of chert, which is similar to flint. It is composed of a dense mass of crystals that range in size from one to ten microns (a micron is a thousandth of a millimeter). No matter how smooth the stones feel, they can be seen through a microscope to be covered with protrusions that scratch away metal. The crystals are interspersed with spaces (pores) that seem to play a role in sharpening, too, because they hold the oil.

Jim Smith says the stones work so well because they "polish while they sharpen." This brings us around to the vagueness of sharpening terms, which need to be sorted out. All the

---

Sharpening
A sampling of techniques and tips

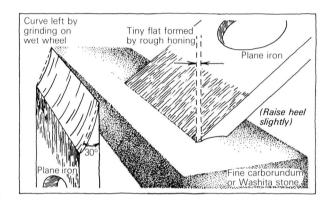

*E*veryone agrees that precise, efficient woodworking is impossible without properly sharpened tools, but there are probably as many ways to get a keen edge as there are practicing craftsmen. The bewildered novice is confronted by a vast array of sharpening equipment and advice, and as the following confirms, there are no absolutes, only preferred ways. Some of the writers are professional woodworkers; others, informed amateurs. All describe what works for them.

The cutting edge
Three steps form the cutting edge: wet grinding, rough honing and fine honing. I feel strongly that dry grinding on any wheel will damage the hardness of the blade edge. Even if you watch carefully and cool the metal in water after each pass, can you definitely say that you have not removed the temper on the terminal .001 in. of the blade, where the edge is actually formed? It seems ridiculous to me to dry-grind a blade and then to use a hard Arkansas stone or to strop the edge afterward. The first cut will dull the edge, and the tool will never cut as well as it would have had it been wet-ground. I even use wet grinding for metal lathe bits and feel it makes a difference. Your blade was carefully heat-treated for a purpose. Don't ruin it.

I use a wet wheel, either manmade or natural, grit from 40 to 100, and turning in either direction to remove the surplus metal, form the edge angle and facilitate resharpening. Edge angles will vary from 2° for a straightedge razor, which is never ground, to 90° for scrapers used to form barrel channels in rifle stocks. My acute-angle block plane, (the only metal plane I use) is ground to around 20° but cuts with the angle up, so blade angle is about 32°. My other planes are about 30°, with 35° for wood chisels. Planer knives are ground to about 30°. Knives should have angles close to 40° but should seldom be ground, with kitchen knives the one exception. No knife should ever show grind or hone marks on the flat of the

blade, but should be tipped well up away from the stone in honing. Scissors and tin snips are ground around 85°.

After grinding, wire edges are removed by rough honing to prepare for the final edge. Many woodworkers abhor a wire edge; instead, welcome it, for after you acquire proficiency, you are only 20 seconds or so away from a shaving edge. Your aim in rough honing is to form a narrow flat (a micro-bevel) along the front edge, using a fairly fine carborundum or Washita stone with thin oil for cutting fluid. I use diesel fuel with a bit of crankcase drainings added. Oil alone is too thick for fast cutting. Set the blade on the stone with both heel and toe touching, raise the heel slightly and lock your wrists to hold that angle. Give the blade a dozen or so strokes, either reciprocating or figure eight, holding the angle constant. Check to see if you have formed a narrow flat; if so, turn the blade over. With the blade flat on the stone, make one stroke toward the edge to remove the wire edge now formed.

The next few strokes are the ones that produce a fine edge with a minimum of effort. Position the blade on the stone, raise the heel as before, and make one stroke toward the edge. Now turn the blade over and make another single stroke with the blade flat on the stone toward the blade edge. Rotating the blade with each stroke, make six or eight single strokes toward the cutting edge on alternate sides of the blade, and you should have a shaving edge. If not, go back to rough honing and try again. From the fine wire edge to the shaving edge takes 5 to 10 seconds if properly done. If you wish, you may repeat the rough and fine honing on an Arkansas stone and/or use a leather strop, but I feel the blade processes of sharpening—grinding, whetting, honing, stropping and polishing—remove metal from an edge by abrasion. All the way down the line to buffing with jeweler's rouge, or stropping on the heel of the hand, the purpose is to get the saw teeth on the edge smaller and smaller. The term "polishing" can be confusing, but in the case of edge tools, "polish" means to produce a bright surface finish by abrasion. The key is always the size of the scratches produced on the edge of the tool.

An 1876 book on grindstones makes it clear: "If we were to examine the surface of a tool that has just been removed from a grindstone, under the lens of a powerful microscope, it would appear as if it were like the rough surface of a field which has been recently scarified with some implement which formed alternate ridges and furrows. . .(the edge) seems to be formed of a system of minute teeth rather than to consist of a smooth edge." The tool, therefore, is ground and polished with finer and finer grit "to reduce the serrature." An Arkansas geologist gave the same sort of explanation. There is no magic in novaculite, he said. The scratches always can be seen through a microscope, no matter how small they are. The fine edge comes from the regularity of the size of the individual crystals in the Arkansas whetstone.

There is also no magic, the geologist said, in the fact that novaculite is mined only in this one spot. The Hot Springs region of Arkansas is interesting geologically, as evidenced by the hot springs, and the fact that it is one of the two best places in the country to find rock crystal, and the fact that Arkansas—alone among the fifty states—has a diamond mine. But other regions are interesting geologically, too, and there is no reason for believing commercial deposits of novaculite will not turn up somewhere else. □

---

fresh from the fine honing will be as sharp as a stropped blade that has made a couple of cuts in hardwood, and you will have wasted the extra time. I realize that in woodcarving, especially in softwoods, a stropped edge may be required, but this is seldom true for planes and chisels. A blade properly fine-honed will shave hair from your arm and will smoothly cut a hard pine knot or rock maple.

To resharpen, repeat the second and third steps until the blade has worn enough to need lengthy honing, with a wide flat on the edge. One could skip the grinding and sharpen solely with the oilstone, but grinding makes it easier and quicker. Another test for sharpness is drawing your thumbnail along the edge with light pressure. If the pull is even along the edge, the blade is sharp. Or hold it in a good light and look for a bright line or spot. If you see one, that part is dull, for a sharp edge is invisible. Check for the wire edge in rough honing by drawing the ball of your thumb along the flat of the blade and out over the edge. If you do not feel the wire edge, it needs more honing.

—*W.A. Haughey, Burlington, Colo.*

Grinding and honing

Many techniques will produce a keen edge; those described here were acquired from a craftsman with over 50 years at the bench. They work well for me. To grind the bevel of a chisel or plane iron preparatory to honing, a good first step is to mark a square edge on the flat side of the blade (with a felt-tip pen, grinding ink or a glasscutter's diamond) as a guideline for the edge. I prefer to mount a ¾-in. by 6-in. medium carborundum grindstone on the lathe, for two reasons. First, the tool rest offers a large and firm bearing surface on which to steady the blade, a real boon for accuracy. Second, low speeds on the order of 1200-1500 rpm can be used, with less danger of drawing the temper. However, grinding on the lathe with an unshielded stone does pose some safety risk, and should be done cautiously and only at low speeds. Patience is a real asset because trying to remove too much steel too fast will draw the temper of the best tool. The slower the better. Never allow a blade to become too hot to hold while grinding; quench frequently in cold water. Do not use oil on the grindstone because it may cause deterioration and crumbling. I check the angle frequently with a protractor bevel; on plane irons, I use an angle of 24° for soft-

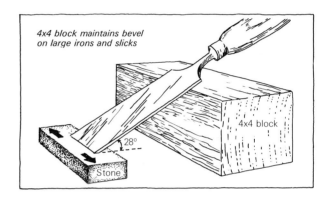

4x4 block maintains bevel on large irons and slicks

4x4 block

28°

Stone

woods, 28° for hardwoods. The blade is passed rapidly and evenly from side to side at the proper angle over the width of the blade until the guideline is reached. Allowing the blade to remain stationary for too long generates heat and usually causes an uneven grind. As a final step, I touch the bevel lightly to the side of the grindstone to take off any high spots.

After grinding to the proper bevel, I remove most of the burr with several heavy strokes on a coarse oilstone with the bevel and the flat side. Then I set to work with a fine India (artificial) stone, using a light penetrating oil. Special oils are sold for honing but I have found those used to free up rusty bolts, such as Liquid Wrench, work just as well. At this point, the woodworker is often advised to rock the iron in a figure-eight movement, holding the heel of the bevel slightly off the stone, in the direction of front to back. I feel this is wrong for several reasons. It is very difficult to maintain a constant acute angle, which is crucial for a keen edge; it produces inequalities over the width of the edge; it causes hollowing of the stone, it is laborious and inefficient. I place the entire bevel absolutely flat on the stone and hone with a constant side-to-side movement, keeping the edge of the iron parallel to the long axis of the stone. I traverse the full length of the stone, changing positions every several strokes, continuing until a highly polished, nearly mirror surface is obtained. Then I reverse the iron and hone the flat side in the same fashion, keeping the entire surface flat on the stone. Honing the flat side of the iron will remove most of the burr, leaving a fine burr on the bevel side. Then I reverse the iron and hone on the bevel, side to side, keeping the bevel absolutely flat on the surface of the stone. Several cycles of alternate honing of bevel and flat side are needed to remove the burr, each cycle shorter as the burr becomes finer. By the time the burr is nearly gone the edge should be keen, and the surface of the bevel mirror-like. The polished surface, however, is irrelevant. The important thing is the edge. A keen edge, when directly illuminated, will not reflect light.

The experienced woodworker uses generous amounts of oil, wiping it off as soon as it becomes black and applying fresh oil. Allowing the porous surface to become glazed will surely ruin a stone. When honing the flat side of the iron, keeping it flat on the stone is mandatory. Honing large plane irons and chisels, such as slicks, can become tiresome. A convenient guide can be made with a heavy block of wood such as a 4x4. Lay the block parallel to the stone and place the bevel on the stone. Move the block toward the stone until the iron rests on the long edge of the block, keeping the bevel flat on the stone. If the block and the stone stay parallel, the angle will be constant and the cutting edge square.

Using an inexpensive artificial stone as above, a satisfactory edge can be obtained, at least for rough work. However, a small white Arkansas stone is a good investment and will produce a fine razor edge. I use it in exactly the same way as the fine India. Only a small amount of honing on the Arkansas should be required for a proper edge.

These techniques do not produce a secondary bevel, or "micro-bevel." This is a personal preference. I feel if the blade is properly ground for its intended purpose in the first place, a micro-bevel isn't necessary. For example, I prefer to have extra plane irons ground for hard and soft woods. I find it harder to produce a razor edge with a secondary bevel because the angle is more difficult to regulate. However, the techniques can be modified during the later stages to produce a secondary bevel if desired. One must keep the heel of the bevel the same distance above the stone during each stroke, though, or the edge will not be keen.

The final stage consists of stropping the bevel and flat side with a piece of leather dressed with jeweler's rouge. The latter can be purchased from jeweler or craftsman supply houses in the form of a bar that is rubbed on the leather. Glue the leather to a block of wood. Strop in the same manner as honing, with the bevel and flat side flat on the leather surface. The edge should not be stropped directly or it will be blunted. The result should be a bevel with a gleaming surface like an old-fashioned razor and a super-fine edge.

—*Daniel A. Symonds, Towson, Md.*

Which way to hone?

When honing on a flat stone, some workers advise moving the tool in a figure eight, some in a straight line back and forth, and some from side to side. I've always been confused by these various instructions, since it seems to me that one way should have something to recommend it over the others. Although I don't have any scientific evidence, logic tells me always to work the tool back and forth over the stone with the cutting edge perpendicular to the direction of honing.

The edge of a tool is a narrow wedge, and most of its work is done by the last few microns of metal. Grinding and honing polish the metal by making smaller and smaller scratches in it. What looks mirror bright to the unaided eye is, under the microscope, an uneven terrain of ridges and gullies. On a tool honed my way, the ridges and gullies run off the edge,

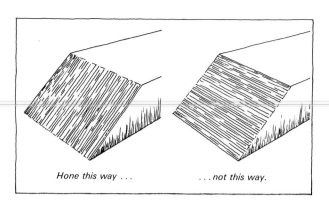

Hone this way . . .   . . .not this way.

which is made up of tiny points supported by a relatively broad base of metal. But on a tool honed the other way, the scratches are parallel to the cutting edge. This seems liable to weaken the very edge you have worked so hard to create. It may break right off in a long sliver of metal, dull after the first cut. So when we have a choice, we should sharpen and hone in the way that leaves these microscopic scratches parallel to the direction of cutting.

—*R. Bruce Hoadley, Amherst, Mass.*

Brush and buff

Over the years I have collected a drawerful of stones, strops and hones. However, I now get along with almost no use of any of them. Instead I sharpen everything (except saws) on a grinder, a wire brush, and a coarse buff. First I shape the tool on the grinder until a wire edge appears, dipping the tool in water more and more frequently as the grinding gets close to the edge. Because the sharpening process is so simple and so little trouble, I feel free to experiment with long bevels, skew chisels, etc., for special purposes. Next I knock off the wire edge on the rotary wire brush. The last step is to charge the buff, which runs at about 2100 rpm, with white emery and proceed to polish the edge. I buff for a short time on the wrong side of chisels to cut off any wire edge that might come with working on the right side. I can shave with anything I sharpen. At the slightest sign of dullness, the tool goes back to the buffing wheel for a few seconds. The buffing wheel is not only faster than the oilstone but also cleaner.

—*John Owen, Isaacs Harbor, N.S.*

Resurfacing stones

Usually, stones become hollow due to long use, but even a new stone may not be really flat. Lack of honing oil can clog or glaze a stone so badly that no amount of rubbing your edge tools on it will have much effect. My early attempts with machine surface-grinding old stones on a silicone-carbide wheel produced a totally useless, glass-smooth surface.

In a short evening I flattened my remaining stones and unglazed the others (eight stones in all) by lapping them. The method is simple: Just pour some kerosene onto a piece of plate glass, sprinkle on about a tablespoon of 60-grit carborundum powder and start rubbing. As the kerosene dries out, add more. When the powder no longer "bites," sprinkle on another spoonful. Rub over the whole surface of the glass to avoid wearing hollows in it. Very fine stones such as Washita or hard Arkansas may be too rough after this treatment, but another minute of lapping on the other side of the glass with kerosene and 220 wet-or-dry silicone-carbide paper removes the roughness. After that, the stone should hone better than ever. Keep on lapping once in a while to prevent your stones from getting hollow again.

—*Rich Baldinger, Schenectady, N.Y.*

Hand grinder

I learned to sharpen tools on a conventional motorized grinder, went over to the sandstone water-trough variety and was finally converted to a hand grinder. The hand grinder does the job well without any chance of ruining the tool and gives a lot of sensitive control over the result. You don't have to worry about the stone disintegrating or softening if kept in water continuously, and it doesn't wear unevenly or crumble. The pronounced hollow grind makes honing a snap. One develops more of a direct, personal relationship with one's tools when they are ground this way, and this probably has a subtle effect on workmanship as well. And a hand grinder is about one-quarter the price of motorized types.

My grinder has a 1:20 ratio. It is model #1107 from Gustav Kunz, 30 Hannover-Wulfel, Volgerstrasse 9m, West Germany. Woodcraft Supply (41 Atlantic Ave., Box 4000, Woburn, Mass. 01888) and Silvo Hardware Company (2205 Richmond St., Philadelphia, Pa. 19125) sell something similar.

I have kept the wheel the grinder comes with, though I discarded the stock tool holder. I also added a few washers to eliminate the disengagement feature of the crank handle.

It was especially bothersome to use a clamp and to have to readjust the tool rest each time, so I glued and screwed a block underneath the mounting board for clamping in my end vise. The rest itself is fastened to the board by two bolts equipped with large butterfly nuts or wing nuts. The heads of these bolts lie countersunk in two slots in the mounting board, so adjusting the rest is a matter of positioning it properly and tightening the nuts. Once made, the adjustment remains when you take the grinder off the bench. When the wheel diameter changes with wear (mine lost 5 mm in two years) or if the angle need be changed (I grind both chisels and plane blades at 26°), a wedge can easily be inserted between the rest and the base. When set up this way, the grinder is always ready for use at a moment's notice.

My tool rest has an optional sliding fence that holds the blades at precisely 90° to the edge of the wheel. Making a slider like this is easy. Most builder's supply stores and hardware stores sell anodized aluminum channel. One length of channel having a base measurement of ⅜ in. and one measuring ⅜ in. between the legs are needed, about 12 in. of the former and 6 in. of the latter. Cut a rabbet in the tool rest slightly deeper than the combined height of the 12-in. piece plus the thickness of the wall of the 6-in. piece. The rabbet should be as wide as the width of the 6-in. channel plus ⅛ in., or about 9/16 in. With wood screws, fasten the long piece, open side up, to the rest. Leave about ⅛ in. between it and the rabbet wall. Bandsaw all but ⅛ in. off the legs on the shorter channel and fasten it to the fence with 4/40 screws. Clearance is important here. Be sure to center the screwheads in the channel. The fence may be made of 3/32-in. plastic, aluminum or brass sheet. Double up on the thickness at the fence edge—use epoxy, first abrading the surfaces. My knob is 2 in. long, held from underneath by two deeply countersunk woodscrews.

The edges of the channels may need breaking or adjusting to permit free sliding. To ensure that the fence edge lies at precisely 90° to the channel guides, hold an accurate try-square against the inset channel and adjust the fence edge to meet its blade exactly. To use this tool rest, turn the wheel toward you with the right hand, while the blade is held lightly against the slider by the thumb of the left. The index finger holds the blade down flat against the surface of the rest and the three remaining fingers rest on the left side of the knob. The index finger also feeds the blade into the rotating wheel as the hand moves back and forth.

—*Alan Marks, Pacific Grove, Calif.*

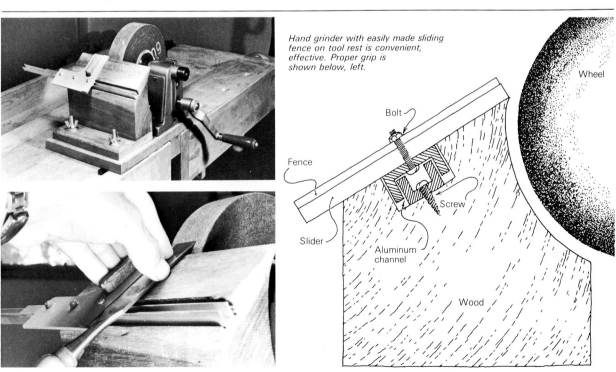

Hand grinder with easily made sliding fence on tool rest is convenient, effective. Proper grip is shown below, left.

Wheel

Bolt

Fence

Screw

Slider

Aluminum channel

Wood

Sharpening Equipment
Our shop tests what's on the market

by Rick Mastelli

Sharpening is a problem for beginning and accomplished woodworkers alike. It's a difficult skill to learn, and early results are usually frustrating. As you come to know what you're doing, it often becomes a reluctant chore. This probably explains why there are so many sharpening gadgets and systems on the market, all advertised as taking the work, the skill, the time-consuming distraction out of sharpening tools, and leaving you with a superior edge. Does any of this equipment do the job? Early this year, the editors of this magazine set out to find out.

We borrowed from the suppliers and manufacturers sharpening equipment of all kinds. We kept this equipment arrayed on a large table in our shop, and for four months we tried it. We sharpened our tools as our woodworking required, and we found ourselves returning to some systems and avoiding others—one indication of their real speed and ease. In addition, I spent hours just wasting metal, trying to find not only the advantages and disadvantages of each system, but also the knack each requires to get the best results. Heretofore my experience with sharpening equipment had been typical: I'd used a high-speed grinder and oilstones. I was intimidated by the grinder for its having ruined by overheating about a third of the edges I'd sharpened, and repelled by the stones because of the mess my oily hands would carry to my wood. Sharpening was a bother I tried to avoid. But in working with these various systems, I learned to enjoy sharpening. The systems didn't make the difference—my concentration did. Even though I didn't get much woodworking done, I found considerable satisfaction in honing my techniques and progressing toward the perfect edge.

For some millenia tools have been sharpened by dragging them across such naturally abrasive stones as sandstone, Belgian clay and novaculite (Arkansas and Washita stones). Although we also have man-made stones today, our bench stones are basically what they've always been. Sometime, somebody got the good idea of spinning the stone, so the tool could be held in one place. He thereby invented grandfather's great treadle-powered sandstone wheel, and that led to today's hand grinder as well as to the high-speed motorized grinder found in most shops. Besides these traditional grinding methods we also have abrasive belts that travel over pulleys, fine-grained Japanese waterstones that rotate horizontally instead of vertically, and slow-speed honing plates that also rotate horizontally, like potter's wheels.

By any method, sharpening is a two-step process. First you form the bevel and shape the edge (usually straight and perpendicular to the sides of the tool), then you hone the edge, polishing and refining it until the very tip disappears. In both stages you are removing metal, and the task is to remove it quickly, accurately and coolly. Overheating the steel ruins its temper, so that the edge, no matter how sharp, won't endure more than a couple of cuts. Some of the systems we tested

perform both operations, some only one, or only one well. What follows is a description of each system and of companion appliances, some subjective conclusions resulting from the hours I spent with them, and at the end, the views of the other two editors who worked with the equipment.

Hand grinders—A hand grinder consists of a vertical wheel powered by a crank; one hand drives the apparatus while the other guides the tool to be sharpened. The large, old-style wheels were often driven directly, while modern versions get a smaller stone up to speed by coupling the crankshaft through a gear train. The old-style wheel ran in a trough of water, to lubricate the cutting and to keep the metal cool.

We tested a 12-in. current-production sandstone wheel, bought at a flea market and jury-rigged, along with two machines that use 1-in. by 6-in. aluminum-oxide grinding wheels, one of them geared up 12-to-1 and the other geared up 22-to-1 (both are sold by Woodcraft Supply, PO Box 4000, Woburn, Mass. 01888, for $31.50 and $64.95 respectively). The wheel of the 22-to-1 grinder clogs less, and the handle disengages to remain still when you're not cranking, but both grinders perform essentially the same. Comparing these to the sandstone wheel, we found, as we expected, that sandstone is simply not as hard as an aluminum-oxide wheel and it does not cut as fast. Also, the wheel-in-water arrangement is messy. Rotating the stone toward the tool is preferred because rotation away tends to draw the metal out, producing a larger burr and a weaker edge, and concentrates heat at the edge instead of directing it toward the tool body, which acts as a heat sink. However, a water-bathed wheel rotating toward you means the tool skims the water off the stone to run down over your hands and onto your feet. I ended up soggily straddling a basin on the floor. Sandstone in water also requires maintenance: You have to drain the trough after each grinding session, or the stone gets soft.

The smaller hand grinders don't have the water problem, and their gear-drives do generate enough speed to remove the metal, barely. If there is much metal to remove, however, and you crank them up fast, they generate more than enough heat to draw the tool's temper. With all three of these wheels, I found hand cranking awkward and tedious, and enough of a distraction to interfere with properly grinding the tool. With so many motorized systems nearby, it was hard for me to resist the temptation to flip a switch when I had grinding to do, and to leave the muscle work to history.

High-speed grinders—The grinding system that is probably most common in shops consists of a coarse and a fine aluminum-oxide wheel attached at either end of the shaft of a ½-HP, 3350-RPM motor. We tested the Sears Craftsman model 9KT 1934C ($124.95); most tool manufacturers offer a similar machine, and a made-in-Taiwan version costs about $50 in

Our test-table here includes hand grinders, tool holders, benchstones and a Sears high-speed grinder with rack-and-pinion grinding fixture. At the front corner of the table are three wheel dressers: a star dresser, a diamond dresser and a carbide shaft. We preferred the last.

discount houses. These grinders waste metal quickly, but generate heat at the same time. The closer you grind to the tool's edge the more gingerly you must proceed, keeping the steel cool by dipping it in water or spraying it with a plant mister, because the thinner metal heats up faster. If you see the back of the tool flash through colors from light straw to true blue, it's too late—the steel has lost its temper. You must painstakingly grind past the surface discoloration, and always at the risk of burning the metal again. If you already own a high-speed grinder, you know the risks, and maybe you've come to terms with burned edges. If you're still shopping for a grinder, consider the gentler systems on the market.

Tool rests—The tool rests that came with the hand grinders and the high-speed grinder don't work well. They're typically a sheet-metal bracket with one leg attached to the machine frame by a nut and bolt in a slotted hole. This permits adjusting the rest's angle and its distance from the wheel. But all too often the near edge of the rest, which should be a useful guide to straightness of grind, is not parallel to the wheel's axis. You have to bend the rest, shim it, or grind it parallel, with little hope of an accurate result—because it's attached at only one point, the rest flexes. Setting such a rest is tedious because there's no fine-tuning adjustment and no way to hold the rest still while tightening the nuts. You need two wrenches, one in a very tight place; at best you get a wing nut, which you can't snug enough to prevent shifting under the vibration of grinding. These rests are really maddening.

One solution is to make your own rest (for an example, see page 69). Another is to use the near edge of the rest (once you've got it parallel to the wheel axis) only as a fence, never bothering about its angle, as shown on page 78.

We also tested two devices for holding the tool at a fixed distance from the wheel while you slide it left and right. The first, from Rima Mfg. Co. (Box 99, Quaker Hill, Ct. 06375), costs $9.95 and sandwiches the tool between two aluminum plates, the lower one of which has a fence that bears against the near edge of the machine's own rest. A similar device

could easily be made of wood. It worked well for extensive grinding, although for touching up an edge, it was faster and easier to control the tool by hand.

The other tool-holding device we tested is a $29.95 gadget made to fit Sears grinders. It has a fine-feed adjustment and rack-and-pinion travel, and it replaces the standard sheet-metal rest rather than jigging off it. In use it flexed, and it was a nuisance to have to unclamp the tool to check the grind. We could never get it back in exactly the same place.

A hybrid—The Advantage model 6150 (pictured on the next page) combines a high-speed grinding wheel, for wasting metal, and a slow-speed waterstone for sharpening. Available from Advantage Machinery Co., 40 White's Pass, South Yarmouth, Mass. 02664, it costs $299.95. It is industrial duty, and its ¾-HP motor can be operated on 110 volts or 220 volts. The 1¾6x7, 60-grit aluminum-oxide wheel rotates at 3600 RPM, and the 1½x8 ceramic waterstone rotates at 144 RPM. The high-speed wheel is essentially the same as the Sears; the waterstone, on the other hand, is a pleasure to use, producing a shallow, hollow-ground bevel without burning the edge. The water and the abrasive combine to produce a slurry that makes grinding more sensitive than it is with a dry, aluminum-oxide wheel. You can press on the tool to feel the circumference of the wheel fit the hollow grind, and cutting will not be wastefully fast, nor will the speed of the wheel, which is heavily geared down, be reduced.

The tool rests are the typical sheet-metal platforms; the one for the waterstone can be mounted on either side of the water trough, for grinding toward or away from the tool's edge. The manufacturer is working on a design for a stiff brush to skim the rim of the wheel and reduce the water that ends up on the floor when grinding toward the edge.

Belt grinders—Belt grinders have several advantages over grinders that use bonded abrasive wheels. Unlike a wheel, a belt doesn't need truing or redressing; you just install a new one when the old one gets loaded and glazed. The length of

The Advantage model 6150 grinding system combines a high-speed aluminum-oxide wheel with a slow-speed waterstone. The first wastes metal quickly, the second sharpens without overheating tool steel.

most belts is at least twice the circumference of most bonded abrasive wheels, which means more surface area to dissipate heat. And you can grind on a belt backed by either a wheel or a platen, for either a hollow or a flat grind.

We tested two belt-grinding systems (below): the Mark II from Woodcraft Supply ($449.95) and the Rockwell model 31-325 ($109.99, without modifications). The Mark II uses an aluminum-oxide belt, 2½ in. wide by 60 in. long, available in grits of 60, 80, 100 and 120. The finer grits clogged easily, and we got the best results from a 60-grit belt. The ½-HP, totally enclosed, 1725-RPM motor drives an 11½-in. dia. main wheel (5635 surface feet per minute) and an 8-in. muslin buffing wheel, both of them running away from the tool edge. The rim of the wheel is slightly convex and made of

high-density polyurethane, which yields a little under pressure, affording a good, sensitive feel of the tool on the belt. It is possible to locate accurately the grinding action on a wide blade by watching where the sparks come from and adjusting the pressure across the width of the tool. Blades up to 2½ in. wide need not be slid across the width of the belt, minimizing variations in positioning and giving you a straight edge. Besides hollow-grind capability, it is easy to fabricate a flat platen of hardwood and to mount it between the main wheel and the idler using hanger bolts through holes drilled in the sheet-steel belt guard.

The Mark II's tool rest is also well designed. Though its angle is fixed, its distance from the wheel is adjustable and determines the bevel angle on the tool. It can accommodate tools up to 24 in. long, is quick and easy to set up and provides consistent, accurate jigging. The rest supports the tool at its butt end, in either a V-trough for chisel handles or in a flat-angled stop for plane-iron ends. This latter could be improved by dressing the crotch with a file to make its hold more secure. Pivoting the tool onto the wheel, rather than sliding it up into it as with a surface-contact tool rest, allows the tool to be placed and pressure to be applied more carefully. It is especially easy to sharpen gouges and other curved-edge tools. That the long belt does not glaze as quickly and dissipates heat better than a bonded abrasive wheel should not be taken to mean that the Mark II cannot overheat tools and ruin their temper; it can. But the design makes it easy to be sensitive to the process and to stop often to cool the tool in water. Repositioning the tool is no problem.

The buffing wheel removes the wire edge left from the grinding belt, polishes the surface and strops the edge. But there is too much give to the muslin. The tool sinks in and the edge is dubbed over. I replaced the muslin wheel with a rubberized abrasive wheel and a solid felt wheel charged with buffing compound. These, being firmer than the muslin, yielded a sharper edge. I came to rely on the Mark II for

The Mark II, above, from Woodcraft Supply, uses a 2½-in. wide aluminum-oxide belt backed by an 11½-in. dia. wheel for grinding and a muslin wheel for buffing. The two bolts at the top of the belt guard hold a hardwood platen we added for flat grinding. The Rockwell model 31-325, right, is fitted with Pro-Edge sharpening attachments. This butt-contact tool rest, like that on the Mark II, is ideal for sharpening curved-edge tools.

quick, accurate grinding, and of all the machines we tested, I used it most often.

The other belt grinder, the Rockwell 31-325, is like a number of consumer-grade sander/grinders by Sears, Montgomery Ward, Belsaw and others. The 31-325 features a narrow 1x42 aluminum-oxide belt that moves at 5000 surface feet per minute over a flat platen. Its 7-in. by 8-in. table offers surface-contact tool support but no jigging facility. It is a noisy, lightweight system, full of vibration, that can be used for sanding and grinding, but is not ideal for sharpening.

A company in the Midwest, Prakto, sells a modified 31-325 and attachments for making it more versatile, accurate and easy to use as a tool sharpener. Prakto adds a reversing switch, an improved tracking knob and sound insulation, though the system is still pretty noisy. The attachments (which fit a number of different makes of sander/grinders) are sold under the trade name Pro-Edge. They include a selection of zirconia-alumina belts (which cut faster and last longer than aluminum oxide), an auxiliary platen (which provides both hollow-grind and flat-grind capability), and a tool holder. This last supports the tool at the butt end. The bevel angle is determined by adjusting the length of the tool holder or by pivoting the entire arm assembly or both—a more complex arrangement than on the Mark II.

The Rockwell with the Prakto modifications and attachments is flimsier and more complicated than the Mark II, but both produce a good edge. The modified 31-325, available from Prakto, 6608 Cottonwood Knoll, West Bloomfield, Mich. 48033, sells for $145. Prakto sells the Pro-Edge attachments for $49.95, a speed controller for $36 and a leather stropping belt for $15. A combination of all their products, including the modified 31-325, is $220.

Motorized Japanese waterstones—These ingenious machines are new on the American market. They consist of a box that houses a motor and gear train, atop of which spins a donut-shaped stone on a vertical axis, like a record player. You grind on the flat, horizontal face of the stone, not on its edge. The stone consists of a fine abrasive suspended in a soft cement that loosens in water. A quart-sized tank sits above the machine, with a valve that trickles water into the hole of the donut stone. Centrifugal force moves the water up the sides of the donut hole and across the stone's working surface in a uniformly thin film. As the stone dampens, and the tool and stone surfaces abrade one another, a slurry forms of stone and metal particles. It takes a while to get used to the working properties of the slurry; it tends to grab the tool and pull it along. But the cut is fast and clean and there is no danger of burning the tool. Centrifugal force continues to introduce fresh water, and to move the slurry over the surface and off the edge of the stone. A collar catches the slurry as it leaves the stone's edge, drains it into a basin, and then it drips out a rubber tube. There are no fierce sparks or harsh grinding noises, but the cool, gentle whir is deceptive, and it takes some practice before the steel you're removing is no more than you want to remove.

We tested three such systems: the Rakuda Standard ($275, pictured above) and Heavy Duty ($495) from Garrett Wade, 161 Ave. of the Americas, New York, N.Y. 10013 (also available from Woodline, 1731 Clement Ave., Alameda, Calif. 94501), and the Makita model 9820-2 ($195, pictured next page). The Rakuda comes with a 1000-grit stone, 8½ in. in di-

The Rakuda Standard motorized Japanese waterstone, from Garrett Wade and Woodline, includes a reservoir from which water drips and is spread over the surface of the stone by centrifugal force. This system removes metal quickly and coolly, leaving a polished surface.

ameter, with a working surface 2⅜ in. wide that rotates at 500 RPM; 100-grit and 2000-grit stones are also available. The Heavy Duty is basically the same as the Standard, except that the stone is 10 in. in diameter, it rotates at 550 RPM, and the top casing is aluminum rather than plastic. It weighs 41 lb., almost twice as much as the Standard, and would hold up well running eight hours a day. For the woodworker who sharpens tools for himself, the Standard is more than adequate. The Makita uses a 7⅛-in. dia. stone with a working surface 2⁷⁄₁₆ in. wide, rotating at 560 RPM. The standard grit is 1000; 60-grit and 6000-grit stones are available.

The flat-grind produced by all three machines is significantly smoother, almost mirror-polished, compared with that produced by a high-speed grinder or by an abrasive belt. This sort of system is thus another hybrid: both grinder and whetstone. Yet it's difficult to actually hone on it, because the metal simply disappears too quickly.

The most significant difference between the two designs is in their tool rests. The Rakuda rest is merely a piece of sheet metal whose height and inclination are fixed by wing nuts. If you take the tool away from the stone to see how much you've ground, it's difficult to get it back where you had it. Finally, I developed freehand control of the tool on the stone. The skill is not so different from that required to sharpen on a stationary stone. The main difference is in the amount of metal removed—the motorized stone is awfully unforgiving of minute discrepancies in your positioning.

The Makita was designed to sharpen planer and jointer knives in addition to hand tools, and the tool rest is a long, machined-steel surface that receives a sliding knife holder and the Rima hand-tool holder (standard equipment) mentioned earlier. The rest is mounted on a pair of columns in the base; height and tilt are adjusted by thumbscrews. The columns are adjusted independently of one another on coarse threads, and there is some play before they are locked down. It is therefore difficult to get the tool rest parallel to the surface of the stone, and to keep it parallel while adjusting height. Similarly, knife-feed adjustment consists not of one thumbscrew, but of four. Each has to be turned the same amount for feed to be even. The standard knife holder will not accommodate planer or jointer knives narrower than 1 in., but a modification is available (at no extra charge, when you purchase the machine) from one Makita dealer: Highland Hardware, 1034 N. Highland Ave. N.E., Atlanta, Ga. 30306. (Makita has since made this modification standard.)

The Makita tool rest is larger, more solid and more useful than the one on the Rakuda machines, though in combination with the Rima hand-tool holder they all produce good results, even if they're tedious to adjust. But the Makita, which is noisier and has a plastic water valve and a plastic collar where the Rakuda has brass and foam rubber, is less enjoyable to use. On the other hand, the Makita is cheaper and more versatile than the Rakuda machines.

Slow-speed hones—Honing removes the wire edge produced in grinding and refines the two surfaces that form the cutting edge. Proponents of hollow grinding hone only a narrow flat, or secondary bevel, at the edge. The Japanese, on the other hand, hone the whole bevel flat and mirror-smooth. In either case, metal is scratched away, just as in grinding, except that the scratches are invisibly small. Traditionally, fine stones have been used for honing; in fact, the Old English word *hán*, from which our word *hone* is derived, means *stone*. After honing, an edge can be kept sharp by stropping, and various materials have been used, including cloth, leather and paper, either alone or charged with abra-

sive powder, and even the palm of the hand. Stropping or honing is the sort of thing you could well do between every few cuts, if it were convenient—consider how often a barber strops his razor. We tested two systems that claim to make honing faster, easier and more effective. Both (pictured on the facing page) employ a horizontal disc that rotates slowly, but neither is actually a hone: One is a motorized strop, the other a slow-speed grinder.

The Xenix Hone is available from Superior Finishes, 7420 Exchange St., Cleveland, Ohio 44125, for $250. It uses a 9-in. dia. wheel of reconstituted leather mixed with rouge in a polyethylene matrix. The wheel rotates at 77 RPM. It is hard, but not unyielding, and so alternately pressing the bevel and the flat of a tool onto its surface slightly dubs over, and thus strengthens, the edge. I found that this machine consistently produced the sharpest, longest lasting edge of any of the systems I tested, except the simple benchstone. It is easy to use, the slow speed is not intimidating, and it requires no tool rest. It is intended to be used often while working, and is available with a foot-operated on/off switch. The beveled surface of the wheel provides clearance for tools like drawknives and its rounded perimeter can be used for stropping the inside of all but the smallest gouges. Rouge added to the leather surface will make it last longer, but the composite itself is abrasive, and as it wears, new abrasive particles are exposed. When the wheel becomes glazed over with metal particles, it can be cleaned with mineral spirits, or you can use mineral spirits to lubricate the wheel as you work. The absorbent surface and slow speed allow no spray off the edge.

The Belsaw Power Hone, model 1019-8, sells for $225 from Belsaw Machinery Co., Equitable Rd., Kansas City, Mo. 64141. Its 8-in. dia. plate is surfaced with 600-grit diamond dust and rotates at 120 RPM. Although this could be a good combination of grit and speed, diamond cuts much faster than other abrasives, and the machine removes metal more quickly than is appropriate for honing. Also, the surface it leaves is visibly scratched rather than polished. On the other hand, to flatten a mis-ground tool back, the plate presents a flatter surface than a stone. The Belsaw is better suited to slow-speed grinding than honing. It will not overheat the tool, though you have to acquire the knack of applying the bare minimum of lubricating fluid because there is no spray shield. The neater procedure is to wipe the spinning plate occasionally with a rag dampened in the lubricant. If the plate gets clogged, it can be cleaned with soap and water.

Benchstones—A benchstone is the most basic of sharpening equipment. I've left these for last not only because a number of the other systems ought to be used in conjunction with benchstones, but also because after all my testing, if I had to choose one and only one system to keep my tools sharp, it would be a good set of benchstones. You can remove metal with benchstones in the quantity a nicked chisel requires, admittedly with the investment of considerable time and effort. But after all, how often do you nick a chisel? In a production shop, where time is a weightier consideration, I would use a grinder, and I would choose the Mark II, but it would supplement my stones, not replace them, and most of my sharpening, especially the final edge, would be done on a stone.

I tested benchstones of four basic kinds: a combination Crystolon/India stone, a Diamond Whetstone, a Washita and hard-Arkansas, and finally a coarse and fine Japanese water-

The Makita 9820-2 is a motorized Japanese waterstone whose tool holder accommodates jointer and planer knives.

The Xenix Hone, left, is a motorized strop, using a slowly rotating plate composed of reconstituted leather mixed with rouge. The plate of the Belsaw Power Hone, above, is studded with 600-grit diamond dust.

stone. The Crystolon/India is made by Norton and sells in most hardware stores for about $15. Both substances are made by fusing an abrasive in a ceramic matrix using an electric furnace; Crystolon is made from silicon carbide, India from aluminum oxide. The particular stone I used combined 100-grit Crystolon with 320-grit India. The Diamond Whetstone (from Diamond Machining Technology, 34 Tower St., Hudson, Mass. 01749) is also man-made though it is not really a stone. It's a perforated steel plate coated with industrial diamond dust and mounted on a plastic block. It comes in grit sizes of 325 and 600, and costs $60 for an 8-in. by 2⅞-in. surface, $34 for a 6-in. by 2-in. surface. Both the Crystolon and the Diamond Whetstone can be used for coarse shaping, as a substitute for grinding; they remove metal quickly enough. For extensive stoning of this sort I found it helpful to use a tool holder; the Eclipse honing guide available from Woodcraft Supply for $11.15 worked well. But it did not make final honing any easier because this process involves sensitively positioning and repositioning the blade alternately on the bevel and flat side. For gross metal removal, diamond is far harder than any other substance, and so it cuts fastest. The Diamond Whetstone also has the advantage of remaining perfectly flat; it will not wear like a stone. In fact, it works very well for flattening worn conventional stones. But even with the fine-grit surface, the diamond cuts so sharply that the scratches are visible, and I could not produce a polished bevel or a very fine edge. The India produced a smoother sur-

face, but this also did not yield the best sharpened edge.

The best edges came from the Arkansas oilstones and the Japanese waterstones. My Washita and hard Arkansas cost $20 and $27 respectively. As is traditional, I lubricate them with a light machine oil cut with various proportions of kerosene, all of which work well. But the most effective lubricant I discovered is a product called Sharp 'N Aid (available from Cannon Valley Mfg., Rt. 1, Cashton, Wisc. 54619 for $2.65 a bottle). It did the best job of keeping the stone from becoming clogged with metal particles. The Washita is a medium-grade hone, and yields an edge equivalent to that produced by the fine India. The hard Arkansas produces a razor-sharp edge that holds up well while cutting.

Japanese waterstones have become my favorite sharpening equipment. The ones I used are from Woodline, though they're also available from Garrett Wade. The coarse (800-grit) stone uses an aluminum-oxide abrasive and costs $11.95; the fine (4000-grit) stone supposedly uses cerium oxide, a fine powder usually used to polish lenses, and costs $12.95. The bonding matrix in each is a soft sort of cement that loosens in water allowing the abrasive particles to move around and re-orient themselves in relation to the tool as it moves over the stone. This action is different from that of a Western stone, where the abrasive particles are held fixed in a denser matrix. Japanese stones polish the metal as well as sharpen the edge. Also, new abrasive particles are continually being freed, so the stone cuts fast and doesn't clog. In addition to the shiny surface they produce, I prefer the touch of waterstones over oilstones. The black hard Arkansas with oil on it is slick and glassy, and you have to restrain your own movements, there's so little friction. The Japanese waterstones, although of finer grit, are more porous, and thus they feel coarser and offer a stabilizing resistance to the movement of the tool. Also, the consistency of the slurry that's formed as the tool and the stone surfaces abrade one another is controlled by the amount of water you add. At first you splash on a lot of water, and the clean stone cuts fast. As you work, you let the surface dry somewhat, and the slurry becomes a fine paste that produces a high polish. Finally you can hear the edge getting sharp. Maybe you can hear it on an oilstone too, but it's not as distinct. The grating sound starts off dull and low and gradually rises in frequency right off the audible scale, and then you know your edge is sharp.

The other reason I like waterstones is that even if I don't thoroughly wipe my hands before returning to my work, I don't bring oily fingers to the wood. □

Prices and availability may have changed since 1981, when this article was first published. However, similar models or good used equipment should be available. Rick Mastelli is video program director at The Taunton Press.

Two other views

I used to look wistfully at the motorized sharpening systems in tool catalogs and think that if I could afford one of these, I could sharpen my tools in less time, with less mess and bother.

The motorized Japanese waterstones seemed most attractive, as they were supposed to yield a finished edge. So I spent several hours trying to hone my chisels. These stones cut so quietly that it was hard to judge how much metal was being removed in only a few seconds. I ended up with a lot of out-of-square edges and multi-faceted bevels.

I was annoyed also by the tendency of the rotating stone to grab the tool. Maybe this was caused by minute changes in the angle of the tool on the stone, whose wet surface would grab when momentary contact was made with the full face of the bevel. But I attributed the grabbing to deposits of ground metal on the stone's surface. I tried wiping them off with a cloth which only soaked up the water and left the gunk behind. I tried wiping the stone with my fingers. This left a nice, clean surface and felt pleasantly like playing in cool mud. The cleaner stone grabbed less; when the deposits would form, I'd wipe them away with my fingers. After an hour, I felt sharp pains in my fingers and noticed blood on the tool. I was horrified to see that I'd ground off several layers of skin, down to the quick flesh. The cool abrasive slush had had an anesthetizing effect, and the damage was done before I knew it. I wore band-aids on my fingertips for several days afterward.

The motorized Japanese waterstones aren't less messy than oilstones, and are more trouble to clean up after use. Their surfaces wear fast and can easily be gouged and grooved by narrow tools. If you're used to moving your body over a stationary stone to sharpen chisels and plane irons, you might find it awkward and difficult to hold the tool in a fixed position while the stone moves underneath it. With practice, however, you can get a nicely honed bevel, but there will be an attenuated burr at the edge, and you won't be able to remove it or to back off the tool properly on the rotating hone. I was always going back to my hard Arkansas stone to touch up the bevel, back-off the tool and remove the wire edge. Of all the sharpening systems that supposedly produced a final edge, the two from Garrett Wade worked the best, but I wouldn't trade my three oilstones for either of them.

Here's why I prefer oilstones: For every series of strokes, I first position the bevel flat on the stone, something that takes a little feeling around to do. You can't feel for this sort of thing on motorized stones, because at the moment the steel touches the abrasive surface, metal starts disappearing. In gaining speed, you sacrifice control, and the adroit touches that make the difference between sharp and razor-sharp.
—*John Lively*

* * *

By the end of our tests, I was satisfied that all of the machines sold as grinders will do that job, once you learn each machine's nuances and quirks. Any of them will shape a satisfactory bevel. Choosing which one to buy thus becomes a matter of pocketbook and of personal taste.

Although I've always used an ordinary high-speed grinder, I liked the motorized Japanese waterstones better because they won't burn the steel, and the abrasive-belt systems best. But at these prices I wouldn't buy either one.

Honing the bevel is another matter. I prefer to grind rarely, but to add a secondary bevel with a medium India benchstone, then to hone that secondary bevel often on a hard Arkansas oilstone. Such an edge is obtained quickly and maintained easily, and it will pare the hair off your arm.

Only two of the test systems—the muslin buff on the Woodcraft Mark II and the Xenix Hone's leather plate—could make a ground edge sharp enough for shaving. But as we worked, I began to suspect that these buffed edges were not as durable as the secondary bevel produced by a fine oilstone. I tested my suspicion by paring a quarter-inch of wood off the ends of 1-by-2 sticks of hard maple, poplar and cherry. I used the same ¾-in. Marples bench chisel, but I ground and rehoned it on different equipment after each bout of paring. Only the oilstoned edge remained sharp enough to continue work after paring all three sticks of wood. Neither buffed edge could complete one stick of wood before requiring a touch-up.

Squinting through a hand lens revealed why. Although buffing polishes the metal, it does not remove the scratches left by the grinder. The buffed edge is fragile, quickly becoming ragged. After a few buffs, you're back at the grinder, taking off another increment of expensive tool steel. The oilstone, on the other hand, takes all the scratches and grooves out for the whole length of the secondary bevel.

Next, I tried preparing the secondary bevel on my oilstone, then maintaining it by buffing. This time, both buffed edges lasted as long as the oilstoned edge. So the buffing wheel has a place: It's best for touching up an edge that's been ground and stoned in the old-fashioned way.

The Xenix Hone produced the sharpest edge of all, but one no more durable than the Mark II. Used in conjunction with oilstones it's a very handy strop. For a carver who must strop his gouges often, the Xenix would be ideal. But as for me, I'll stick to my cheap Sears grinder and my trusty oilstones.
—*John Kelsey*

Slow-Speed Sharpening
Lessening the chance of burning your tools

by Mark White

To reduce the risk of friction-caused heat drawing the temper of my tools, I designed a simple-to-make sharpening system that incorporates a vertical shaft turning slower than 300 RPM. The horizontal wheel, which allows flat grinding rather than hollow, may be a conventional grindstone or a flat wooden plate covered with an abrasive disc. For stropping, I use a crowned wooden disc covered with leather and charged with an abrasive compound.

The heart of the system, shown below left, is a laminated disc bolted to a standard pipe flange, which is in turn screwed to a short length of 1¼-in. pipe. The pipe turns in two bearings made of 4-in. by 4-in. by 9-in. chunks of hickory. I bored the holes for the bearings with an adjustable bit set to bore about 1/16 in. larger than the pipe's diameter, to compensate for swelling of the block and tightening of the hole when oiled. If you drill oversize and experience wobble in the shaft, you can cant the blocks until they bear upon the shaft. The hole in the upper block should pass entirely through it. The lower block should be drilled 1 in. short of going through, so that the shaft has a full inch of wood to rest on as it turns.

To make the pulley, I bandsawed two 14-in. discs and one 12-in. disc from

⅝-in. plywood. I marked and drilled the centers of these discs to take a ⅜-in. bolt and used these center holes to position the discs during glue-up, sandwiching the smaller disc between the two larger ones.

Next I lag-bolted the bearing blocks to the front edge of my workbench, lubricated them with chainsaw oil and inserted the pipe with pipe flange. I positioned the laminated pulley on top of the flange, and marked, drilled and bolted it in place.

The vertical-shaft motor I took from a junked washing machine. I mounted the motor on the workbench, hooked it up to the pulley and let it run for about 30 minutes in order to wear in the hickory bearings. The face of the flange did not run perpendicular to the axis of rotation, but a bit of fiddling with a couple of cardboard shims between the pulley and the flange leveled the disc.

A conventional grindstone could be mounted right on the pulley, but I chose to use my system for stropping. I stacked and glued a few more plywood discs to the top of the pulley, switched on the motor and turned the head with a sharp gouge to a rounded, conical shape. (Leather yields under pressure, and if the leather were applied to a flat surface, a tool pressed to the leather

would sink in and the tool bevel would become convex.) Sanding completed the shaping of the head, and a heavy coat of paint sealed the wood. From a local leather shop I picked up a piece of 3/16-in. thick shoe-sole leather, soaked it in hot water and molded it in place over the head. A nut and washer hold the leather in the center, and a ring of aluminum tacks holds down the perimeter. The leather can be charged with various grits of aluminum-oxide buffing compound; the distance you hold the tool from the center of the disc also affects the speed of the sharpening action. Because the head is crowned slightly, wide-edge tools are easier to sharpen. Attention can be concentrated on a small section of the edge, while the ends clear the perimeter and hub of the wheel. Always hold the tool on the plate so the rotation is away from the cutting edge; otherwise the tool can grab and cut the leather.

The system can be varied to incorporate a large flexible sanding disc which, if run at 800 RPM would be useful for sharpening axes, adzes and drawknives. A reversible motor would be useful for knives and other two-edge tools. □

Mark White teaches woodworking in Kodiak, Alaska.

White's horizontal sharpening system, which rotates at only 300 RPM, can be fit with a grindstone, an abrasive disc or a leather-covered stropping wheel. An old washing-machine motor provides power.

Another of White's slow-speed sharpening arrangements has a 2-in. by 9-in. aluminum-oxide wheel on a ¾-in. mandrel powered by a 1,725-RPM motor. A 3-in. pulley at the motor and a 10-in. pulley at the mandrel yield a grindstone speed of about 500 RPM, fast enough to remove metal with reduced risk of burning the tool.

Grinding
Use your tool rest only as a fence

by Frank Klausz

Grinding is the first step in shaping the bevel on a cutting tool. It makes the edge straight and square and puts the bevel at the proper angle. It is not necessary to regrind every time you sharpen; a properly ground edge can be honed many times. I grind damaged tools and new tools that have been incorrectly ground. I also regrind tools after repeated sharpening has flattened the hollow grind; it's easier to hone a hollow grind. In my apprentice years, we did not use a motorized grinding wheel. We had a flat, rough whetstone about 8 in. by 4 in. by 3 in. that sat in a wooden basin with a couple of inches of water. I spent many hours at that stone, and every week the worst job in the shop was to change the water and clean out the wooden basin so you could see the bottom. Flat grinding on such a waterstone and honing on a fine, grey stone produces the best edge, and it holds up longer than a hollow-ground edge, but if you have to remove a lot of metal, it takes a long time to do and a lot of sweat.

For faster, easier grinding, use an electric grinder with a 60-grit aluminum-oxide wheel, rotating toward you at 3,000 RPM. I prefer a 1-in. or wider wheel at least 6 in. in diameter. Wheels smaller than 4 in. in diameter give too deep a hollow grind. I keep the wheel clean and dressed with a carborundum block; a glazed stone will not cut well, and can overheat the tool. My grinder has a cover around the back of the wheel and a transparent shield on top. I get gooseflesh when I see a grindstone spinning freely with no cover and no safety glass for the operator. Protect your eyes.

My grinder also has a standard tool rest whose angle and closeness to the wheel are adjustable. But I never change it. The only part of the tool rest I use is the lower edge, as a guide for my right index finger. The tool need not lay flat against the surface of the tool rest. If it did, you'd have to adjust it for each tool, depending on the steel and the work. Less dense woods require more acute angles, and hard steel can hold its edge ground to such smaller angles. Chisel and plane blades should be ground to 25° or 30°. To determine these angles, compare the width of the bevel with the thickness of the blade. The face of a 30° bevel is twice as wide as the thickness of the blade; a 25° bevel is two and one-third times as wide as the thickness of the blade. By the time you get the tool-rest angle right, you can have finished grinding, if you use the tool rest only as a one-point guide.

Hold the blade in your right hand between your index finger and thumb, about in the middle of the blade. Lay the tool on the tool rest and bring the edge toward the wheel until your index finger touches the back edge of the tool rest. If the wheel touches only the tip of the blade, move your finger down a bit. If the wheel touches the blade before your finger touches the tool rest, move your finger up a bit. Once you've found the right place, keep your finger there and use it as a stop to slide against the tool rest. Move the blade right and left, applying light pressure on the blade with the fingers of your left hand. There are only two supports for the blade— the index finger at the bottom edge of the tool rest and the wheel itself. This ensures that the hollow grind will be even. Keep the blade moving back and forth across the wheel and dip the edge often in water. When the beads of water on the tool evaporate, dip again. Don't get any blue mark on the chisel because that means you have raised its temperature to where it has lost its temper and however sharp an edge you get, it will dull easily. As the grind nears the edge of the tool, the danger of burning increases because the thin metal heats up fast. This metal will be your cutting edge and its temper is critical. You should get sure enough of the position of the blade in your right hand to be able to free your left hand to spray the edge with water from a spray bottle as you grind. It takes practice, but no jig will provide the feelings you will learn to recognize when you are grinding properly. □

Frank Klausz, who was trained as a master cabinetmaker in his native Hungary, now builds and restores furniture at his shop in Bedminster, N.J.

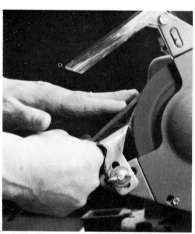

The proper position for the index finger of the right hand, which rides against the bottom of the tool rest, will produce an initial grind mark about in the middle of the bevel, left. If the grind mark is too high, lower your finger; if the mark is too low, raise your finger. While grinding, second photo from left, the blade does not necessarily rest on the flat of the tool rest; the position of the index finger determines the bevel angle. As the grind nears the edge of the blade, it becomes easy to overheat it. Learn to control the tool with only your right hand, freeing your left to spray the edge with water as you grind, second photo from right. At right, the hollow-ground bevel directly off the grinder.

How to Sharpen
A keen edge makes all the difference

by Ian J. Kirby

Putting the cutting edge on a chisel or plane iron causes confusion, doubt and fear in many beginning woodworkers. Yet once the tool's edge has been ground (to the appropriate angle and square to its long edges), sharpening takes only about one minute. A sharp tool is the difference between despair and delight—you need to sharpen often and without any fuss. After sharpening, a plane not only feels different as it cuts, it also sounds different—when it's blunt it cuts with a dull and heavy tone, but when it's sharp it sings.

What is it we have to do by sharpening? The diagram below shows a magnified section through a blade. The rounded edge at A is blunt; B, with the surfaces meeting at a straight line, is sharp. If we remove metal in the shaded area (C), we will have a sharp edge. But if we first grind the tool to a 25° angle and then sharpen to a 35° angle, we can accomplish the same thing more efficiently by removing a very tiny amount of metal (D). The grind can be hollow or flat; it matters little. What does matter is the 35° sharpening angle. The amount of metal we have to remove is measured in angstroms—at most, a few thousandths of an inch. In order to sharpen the blade, there is really very little work to do.

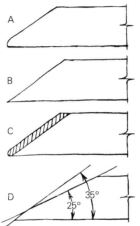

For chisels or plane irons, the sharpening grip is the same. Grasp the blade in the right hand, far enough forward to plant the index finger atop the edge (above left). This hand holds the iron and provides both power and pressure. Then make an L of the left hand, place the fingers atop the blade, and the thumb underneath (above right). This hand holds the angle, and also provides controlled pressure. This grip thus allows you to maintain and control both angle and pressure. Most left-handers find they can adopt this grip without reversing hands. Stand with your feet apart, parallel to the edge of the sharpening bench but far enough away to throw your shoulders forward, knees flexed slightly (photo below). Lock your wrists to maintain the sharpening angle as you move the iron forward and back on the stone. A wooden angle block, shown on table, can be used to check your position.

The important considerations in learning how to sharpen are how to hold the tool, how and where to stand, and how to use your body to move the tool over the stone. The photos at right give these answers. One of the things we have to achieve is controlled pressure across the cutting edge; the other necessary control is maintaining the constant angle between blade and stone. The grip shown in the photos provides both of these controls. With either chisel or plane iron, the index fingers of both hands are on top of the tool. Pressure can be exerted uniformly, or on one side of the blade or on the other side—whatever the tool requires. Angular control also comes from this two-hand grip, from the wrists, and subsequently from the shoulders, but the key to it is the thumb of the left hand. It acts as a fulcrum or back rest, and with the hand spread this way it is easy to keep the left thumb solidly locked in position. You find the angle in the first place by feeling for the grinding bevel, or by checking against a block of wood cut to 35°. Then, the left hand becomes a very sensitive jig.

What kind of stone is best? The type of stone you use is a matter of preference. You really need only two stones, a medium and a fine, provided you have some other way of grinding the edge (and if not, a coarse stone and some elbow grease will do it). They can be either oilstones or waterstones, although it's unwise to have one of each. The function of the

The main difference between sharpening a chisel and a plane iron is the pressure applied to the tool. The hand position, as shown in the two photos at right, is basically the same. Bear down hard on the wide iron, varying the pressure from left to right every few strokes, to round the edge slightly. Maintain constant, light pressure on a narrow tool. Here, Kirby uses a Japanese waterstone, kept wet by squirts from a plant sprayer.

lubricant is to keep the edge of the tool cool, to smooth the sharpening action, and to float away metal and stone debris, thereby helping to prevent plugging or glazing of the stone's abrasive surface. If you have oilstones, the type of oil is also a matter of preference. A light machine oil such as 3-in-1 is good. Motor oil cut with kerosene is popular, and straight kerosene is suitable on a fine stone.

The bench or shelf on which you keep your sharpening stones is a vital element of the workshop. It should be sturdy and built for the job. The surface should be easy to clean—Formica is ideal. There should be a cover over the whole thing or else covers for the individual stones, to protect them from dust, which clogs them and destroys their cutting action. Choose a bench height to suit your own body—34 in. is a good place to start. The stones should be mounted with their long ends at right angles to the front of the bench, and held firmly in place between small blocks fastened to the bench. When planning the bench, don't forget that you need about 10 in. to the right of each stone to clear the tool handle when backing off. Keeping stones in a toolbox is not good practice because sharpening is too important and too frequent an operation to be hindered by having to dig them out and set up some temporary work station. It's also bad to spill dirty water or oil on your workbench.

How much pressure to exert? The pressure varies with the blade you are sharpening—the wider the iron, the more pressure. With a 2⅝-in. plane iron, apply almost as much pressure as you can deliver, while still being able to move. With a ¼-in. chisel, apply very little pressure. The ¼-in. chisel is probably the most difficult tool to sharpen while retaining the right-angularity of the edge, and the usual fault is too much pressure. With narrow tools, you must take care to move around on the surface of the stone as you sharpen, to keep from wearing a groove in it. Some people avoid this problem by turning the stone on its edge.

Should the tool be held askew to the long edges of the stone? If the blade is narrower than the stone, you should keep the edge at right angles to the edge of the stone and to its direction of travel. In this way you will have to consider and practice a uniform grip and stance, and you will be more likely to get uniform results. Wear on the stone will be more even, and sharpening time will be minimized. When sharpening a plane iron that is wider than the stone, it's common to sharpen aslant, so the whole edge is on the stone. However, because plane irons are usually sharpened with a very slight

curve, more pressure is exerted on the left side of the iron for a half-dozen strokes, then on the right for a half-dozen strokes.

How long a stroke do I take? Learn to use the whole length of the stone, reversing direction an inch or so from each end. This keeps the stone flatter and speeds the process along. Maintain the pressure in both directions, forward and back.

How do I know when to stop? If you visualize what you are trying to do, you'll realize that once you've removed the face of metal that includes the rounded portion, then the edge is sharp. However, you can't know when this has been achieved, so you go a bit beyond. The effect is that the unsupported metal at the very tip of the edge collapses and bends over—a burr or wire edge forms. When you can feel the burr by running your thumb off the flat side (back) of the blade, it's time to stop. Now, turn the blade over flat on the stone and remove the burr by "backing off." No matter what, keep the back of the tool flat on the stone. If you lift the tool to an angle to remove the burr, you've changed the sharpening angle. Correcting the fault wastes both time and metal.

Backing off should be done only on the fine stone. The sequence of events, if all goes well, is this: Sharpen on a medium stone at a 35° angle until you just detect the burr, go to the fine stone and sharpen at 35° until you have polished out the scratches left by the medium stone, turn the blade over and back off. Don't back off on the medium stone before going to the fine stone, it's an unnecessary step. The back of the chisel or plane iron should touch only your finest stone.

There is no need to raise a huge burr, although it's possible to sharpen to the point where, as you back off, a visible wire of metal detaches itself. This may look impressive but actually you've removed about five sharpenings worth of metal, shortening the life of the grinding angle. You should expect to get 20 or 25 sharpenings between grindings, the first taking the fewest strokes, the second a few more, and so on.

What if, after backing off, the burr is now on the beveled (face) side? It frequently happens that way, and you simply turn the tool over, take a few light strokes, then back off again. You must persevere until, when running the thumb off either side of the blade, no burr can be felt.

How do I know the blade is sharp? There are two simple ways. A 10-power or 15-power hand-lens should be part of every woodworker's tool kit. A look through the lens at this stage is dramatic. What you thought to be a smooth surface turns out to be something like the surface of a worn phonograph record. With ×15 magnification you'll be able to see

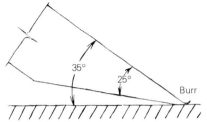

Sharpen at a 35° angle (right) until you detect a burr. Turn the tool over and back off on a fine stone. When backing off, the iron must lie flat on the stone (as shown at left and above). Use the fingers of both hands to press it down evenly.

whether the edge is a clear intersection between the sharpening angle and the back side of the blade. The other way to check is to feel that there is no burr on either side of the blade, then to offer the tool very carefully and gently to your thumbnail, as shown in the photograph below. The lower the angle you can achieve between thumbnail and sharpened edge, the sharper it is. This may seem dangerous but it has plenty of historic precedent: Silversmiths and engravers use the method to check the edge on gravers, and metal-lathe operators frequently employ it too. If you're still uneasy about pointing a sharp edge at your cuticle, set your thumbnail vertically on the bench and approach from the knuckle side.

If you are shopping for stones, I'd suggest a medium India (a man-made stone) from a reputable firm like Norton or Carborundum. For the fine stone, I strongly recommend that you use a soft or hard Arkansas. It is best if both stones are the same size and not too small—9 in. by 2½ in. is ample. If a large Arkansas is too expensive, get the largest you can afford. These two stones will last the rest of your life.

Japanese waterstones are gaining popularity. Although the edge produced by an Arkansas oilstone has long been a standard of sharpness, I find the waterstone to be even bet-

ter—another level of quality that's really quite extraordinary. Japanese waterstones come with instructions for care and maintenance; they're used the same way as oilstones, and again, a medium and a fine stone are all you require.

Whatever the stone, unless it's kept flat in its length and its width, it's of little use. To check, clean and dry the stone by pressing it into a paper towel, then hold it to the light against a straightedge, just as you would check a piece of wood. If the length shows a hollow of 1/32 in. or more, or if you see any hollowing in the width, it's time to flatten.

Flattening a waterstone is simple. Place a piece of plate glass about 20 in. square on a flat surface. On it put a piece of 220-grit wet/dry sandpaper. Flood the paper and the stone with water, and grind the stone on the paper using as much of the paper's area as you can. Wash the stone and paper often by dipping them into a bucket of water, and dry the stone before you check it with a straightedge.

To flatten an oilstone, use a different piece of plate glass in a similar way. Sprinkle about ¼ cup of 80-grit carborundum powder (available from lapidary shops) onto the center of the glass, and pour about ¼ cup of water into the grit. Grind the stone in a circular motion, using as much of the glass area as

At left, the sharp edge. Find out how sharp by gently offering the blade to your thumbnail, below. The lower the angle at which it will catch, the sharper it is. At right, the sharpening bench in Kirby's shop is sturdy and easy to clean.

you can. Keep heavy pressure on the stone as you grind. It's easiest to flatten your coarser stone first, while the grit is cutting fastest; a fine Arkansas can take a long time to flatten, especially if it's been allowed to become much hollowed. To check the stone, scrape off the grit slurry, wash the stone, dry by pressing into a paper towel and test with a straightedge. After flattening a dozen stones, you'll probably notice the glass becoming hollow. Get a new piece of glass.

Problem tools. The spokeshave is awkward to sharpen because of its short blade. You can do it by holding it in your fingers but a better way is to make a wooden block about 5 in. by 2 in. by ¾ in. Saw a kerf in the end so that the spokeshave blade can be inserted about an inch into the block. You'll be able to exert ample pressure and still keep good control.

Carving tools can be sorted into three types: flat chisels, gouges and veining tools. Flat chisels are sharpened like bench chisels but on both sides. Thus to keep the same 35° angle you'd have to shoot for 17°30′ on each side, practically impossible. Since carving is such a variable process, just sharpen on one side until a burr is raised and then sharpen from the other side. A carving chisel usually has to be sharpened more often than a bench chisel.

The carving gouge is held the same way as a bench chisel but people often move it in a figure eight across the stone, rolling it as they go, to sharpen each part of the edge. A disadvantage of this method is that wear in the center of the stone is double, and it's soon hollowed. I find it better to work in a straight line along one edge of the stone, or with the stone turned up on edge, rolling the gouge to reach its whole edge. Once a burr has been raised on the inside, you'll need a slipstone to deal with it. Slipstones are usually small and handheld, not mounted. They're made in a variety of shapes, from flat like a miniature oilstone to cylindrical to conical with a conical hollow on the back side. The conical sort is most common, but cylinders are more useful, although you'll need a variety of cylinders to fit a variety of gouges. Most carvers collect them over the years, the same way they collect gouges. Choose a slip of smaller radius than the gouge, and work it flat on the inside face of the gouge to remove the burr.

An in-cannel gouge is a special problem calling for a cylindrical stone of its exact radius. Brace the butt of the gouge on the bench and work the slip in and out, rotating it at the same time, and maintaining the 35° angle with the tool's back. Then backing off can be done on a normal flat stone.

V-tools and veiners are similar to flat chisels, and most of the trouble comes on the inside, where the two faces meet. First sharpen both outside faces on a flat stone in the usual way, but then to remove the burr from the inside you'll need a stone shaped to an angle that will reach the bottom of the V. Usually a small slip can be ground to the necessary angle.

Many carvers avoid the problem by buffing their tools on a cloth wheel charged with rouge or tripoli. This will produce an extremely sharp edge, but it's haphazard and offers little control of angle. It's also difficult to shape a wheel so it will fit inside a gouge or V-tool. This lack of control usually does not matter to the carver, but the cabinetmaker needs precise angular control and an absolutely flat back, and for these reasons I advise against buffing. It's cheaper, easier and better to learn how to sharpen on flat stones. □

Ian J. Kirby teaches woodworking and furniture design at Kirby Studios, Cumming, Ga.

Japanese Blades
Traditional sharpening methods

by Toshio Odate

Although most woodworking apprentices begin training at the age of 13 or 14 years, I was 16 when my parents decided I should apprentice to a *tategu-shi*, the craftsman who makes doors, *shoji* (screens) and room-dividing panels. My starting master was my stepfather, which was unusual. It was common to be sent to apprentice with another craftsman for at least the first two to three years for spiritual as well as technical training. My stepfather was very strict and believed a father could not teach his own son. The first day he said to me, "From this day on we are total strangers. I will treat you like a common apprentice, maybe harder. You should call me master, not father." He did as he said.

A *tategu-shi* apprenticeship lasts five years. Two additional years, the first and last, are done as a service to the master, extending the relationship to seven years. The first year is spent working in the household and studio doing errands and assisting the master's wife. At this time you are beginning to learn the manners and attitudes of a craftsman through observation. The seventh year is spent working as a craftsman without salary to show appreciation to your master.

An experience in my third year that is still important to me helps to illustrate the relationship a craftsman has with his tools. I had saved a little pocket money given to me by my master and other craftsmen for doing errands. But as my daily needs were taken care of by the master, there was little reason to have or spend money. On the first and fifteenth day of the month we would take a half day off, but only after the master's tools and my tools were taken care of and the shop was cleaned. I was finally free around two o'clock. You can imagine just how precious those hours were to me. One afternoon I took the train to a store that was well known for its fine tools. There I purchased a plane that had been made by a famous blacksmith. At the time I did not know his name or the fine quality of his tools. All I knew was that the plane was expensive. On the train I was so overjoyed I unwrapped the plane and held and looked at it all the way home. I knew I couldn't show the plane to anyone because people would laugh at me—I was still a novice. I couldn't even keep it in my toolbox for fear someone would see it. I enjoyed the plane every evening while in my room. After the lights were turned out, I kept the plane by my bedside.

One day it was raining, and everyone was fixing tools. I don't remember why—it wasn't a day off—but my plane was now in my toolbox. I was pretending to fix my tools but was really looking at my plane. All of a sudden my master was standing behind me. It was too late. He asked, and I had to tell him I had bought it. He took the plane and showed it to the other craftsmen. They, too, thought it was a wonderful tool but teased me because I still did not know how to appreciate its greatness. They took the blade out of the block and examined it carefully. They talked about it for a long time, then gave it back to my master. My master came to me holding the plane in his hand and told me simply that the plane was too good for me. He took it away, and I never saw it again. I had expected that to happen.

Tools are made to be used, and great tools have to be used by great craftsmen. The plane was not for me and should not have been mine only to keep in a cabinet. I should have had greater respect for the tool and the craftsman who made it. It was a very painful and expensive lesson, but I learned.

Sharpening Japanese blades—Most Japanese woodworking tool blades are made by laminating steel (figure 1). High-quality Western blades also used to be made this way. The edge of the blade is thin and extremely hard and is supported by a thick, soft steel. The center of the back of the blade is hollowed-out to facilitate keeping the back completely flat. Most blades are beveled on one side, except for ax-like tools, which are beveled on both sides with hard steel laminated in the center. Plane blades, chisels and knives are made in the same manner, and the methods for sharpening them are similar. Once you have learned the techniques of sharpening plane blades, which are the most complicated, you will be able to sharpen any flat blade.

A new plane is usually ready to use, but most Japanese craftsmen will recondition it to suit their own preference. The optimal bevel angle depends on the quality of the blade and on the kind of work you are doing. Until you know otherwise, it is best to maintain the original bevel angle of the blade.

If the edge of the blade is not finished when purchased or is badly chipped, a grinder can be used to start the sharpening process. When I worked in Japan I did not have a grinder and always used a coarse stone, as was the custom. Mechanical tools were generally not used. Today a wide variety of machines and tools is available to make dressing or redressing a blade faster and more accurate, but sharpening itself, honing the final edge, has to be done by hand.

There are oilstones and there are waterstones; in Japan we used only waterstones. Many Japanese craftsmen prefer natural stone, but it is difficult to find large stones that have an even consistency. Today, manufactured stones are readily available at an affordable price. Three stones (coarse, medium and fine) are needed. When sharpening (and not redressing) a blade, only the medium and finishing stones are used.

When using a waterstone, water must be added constantly, or the pores of the stone will clog. Keeping the surface of the stone clean gives a faster grind. Japanese craftsmen keep a bucket of water next to the stone, or they have a sink-like wooden box beneath the stone (figure 2).

In sharpening, be sure to wipe the blade before changing to a finer grade stone to keep from transferring coarse particles. Before changing stones you should allow the stone you're on to dry during the last few strokes. This results in a smooth transition to the next stone. As the stone dries, the pores of the stone clog slightly, thus acting as an intermediate grit.

How the blade is held during sharpening is important. The plane blade is held in the palm of the right hand with the index finger extended (photos, right). Place the first two or three fingers (depending upon the size of the blade) of your left hand in the space created by the right thumb and index finger. Your fingers will maintain pressure on the blade so as to steady the bevel. The left thumb, placed under the blade, will provide support for the back.

The angle of the blade on the stone has to be constant

Fig. 1: Blade structure

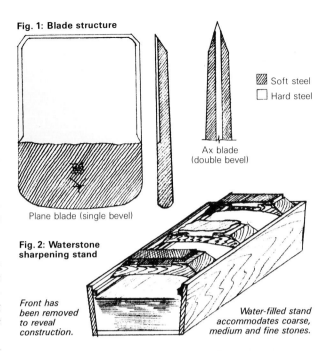

Soft steel
Hard steel

Ax blade
(double bevel)

Plane blade (single bevel)

Fig. 2: Waterstone sharpening stand

Front has been removed to reveal construction.

Water-filled stand accommodates coarse, medium and fine stones.

To sharpen the bevel, hold the blade in the right hand, index finger extended to press in back of the bevel. The fingers of the left hand fit between the index finger and thumb of the right hand, also pressing in back of the bevel. Position the thumb of the left hand to support the blade at the back. Keep the angle of the blade on the stone constant while rubbing back and forth.

Drawings: Toshio Odate

Planes and Chisels **83**

Fig. 3: Bevels

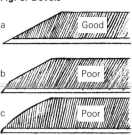

a — Good
b — Poor
c — Poor
d — Poor

Fig. 4: Plane-blade bevel

A plane blade must be sharpened flat from the edge to the top of the bevel but slightly convex across its width, to keep the corners from digging in. Roughing-plane blades should be more convex than smoothing-plane blades. The convexity shown is exaggerated for illustration.

When a burr has been raised on the flat side of the blade from sharpening the bevel on the medium and fine stones, flip the blade over and hold it with the fingers of the right hand around the back and the thumb extended to press on top of the bevel. Lay the blade flat on the fine stone and bring the thumb and fingers of your left hand to bear on the corners of the bevel. Rub hard back and forth until the burr has been bent back to the bevel side. Continue to rub the blade alternately on the bevel and the flat side until the wire edge falls off.

while sharpening; the surface from the edge of the blade to the top of the bevel must be perfectly flat (figure 3a). This is particularly important for chisels, which are sometimes used like planes, with the bevel riding on the wood—the flatness and smoothness of the bevel help to control the cut and also contribute to the strength of the edge. A double bevel or a convex bevel (figures 3b and 3c) will cause plane blades to skip when cutting hard grain or knots. If the beveled surface is slightly concave (figure 3d), maximum control and also support for the fragile hard-steel edge are sacrificed. Hollow-ground bevels are easier to hone, but there are disadvantages: They do not produce the strongest edge, and they are especially bad for laminated blades.

While the bevel must be perfectly flat from the edge to the top, plane blades require additional shaping: The edge must be slightly convex (figure 4) to prevent the corners of the blade from cutting into the planed surface. The shape is produced by subtly varying the pressure on the blade from side to side during the stroke. The convexity of the edge of a roughing-plane blade should be more pronounced than that of a smoothing-plane blade.

Japanese craftsmen sharpen not on a bench, but with their stone, or their stone stand, on the floor. The squatting position allows you to bring your weight to bear on the work. The orientation of the blade on the stone depends on the size of the blade and the training of the craftsman. Some craftsmen

are taught to sharpen with the edge of the blade always perpendicular to the stroke. This probably produces the strongest edge, but it requires keeping the elbows in close to the body, not their most natural position. I usually sharpen with the blade angled at about 30° to the stroke. This allows me to lock my hands and wrists and still move freely from the upper arms. Another advantage of this position is that it provides greater support for the bevel on the stone to steady the angle during the stroke. The greatest support comes from holding the blade parallel to the direction of the stroke; then there's little chance of rocking the bevel. To hold the blade this way, the stone must be at bench height, and you stand alongside the stone, rather than behind it. I use this position for very thin blades and also for gouges.

The blade should be sharpened on the coarse or medium stone, rubbing back and forth until a burr appears across the edge. To detect the burr, rub the back of the blade gently with your finger; it should not be quite visible. Switching to the finishing stone, sharpen in the same manner until the whole bevel is mirror-smooth. Turn the blade over and hold it with the fingers of your right hand around the back and your thumb extended to press on the top of the bevel. Bridge this thumb with the fingers and thumb of the left hand, pressing on the corners of the blade (photo, left). Rub 15 to 20 times with the back flat on the stone until you can feel the burr bent back to the bevel side. It is important not to sharpen the back of the blade until this time, and only on the finishing stone. Repeat the finishing process back and front until the burr falls off. Resist the temptation to peel the burr off as this will leave a raw edge. Sharpening is now complete.

Maintaining the flat back—The back surface of Japanese blades is unique in that the flat between the hollow grind and the blade edge is extremely narrow. It is common knowledge among Japanese craftsmen that the blade performs best just when this flat is narrowest. After repeated sharpenings finally make the flat disappear, a new flat has to be created. If the blade is wider than ⅜ in., Japanese craftsmen usually strike the edge of the soft steel with the corner of a small hammer on the bevel side of the back so as to bend the steel down slightly. It requires considerable skill to do this right because the hard steel of the back of the blade can crack from the slightest vibration of a misdirected blow. Most Japanese craftsmen have had this experience, including myself. I can remember hiding a blade from my master. If one wants to acquire the skill, one must take the chance and practice. I prefer using the corner of a hard wooden block, but some use the corner of an anvil. Either way, place the back of the blade on the corner, making contact ¼ in. to ⅜ in. down from the edge in the middle of the blade, exactly opposite where you will strike with your hammer. Tap lightly and repeatedly along the center two-thirds of the width of the blade (photos, opposite page), moving the blade between taps to position the corner underneath the hammer. Depending on the thickness of the blade, 15 to 25 taps should push out the hollow in the back enough to produce a flat at the edge after grinding.

Grinding is accomplished with a flat steel plate 2 in. by 8 in. by ¼ in. (stones are not flat enough), a pinch of carborundum powder (silicone carbide grain, grit #46) and a few drops of water. Mix the carborundum and water on the steel plate and rub the back of the blade, giving little pressure at the beginning, keeping the carborundum paste under the

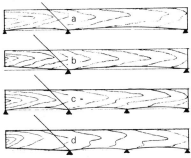

Fig. 5: Plane-sole contours

For truing (a), the sole is relieved so the plane contacts the work only at the front, the blade and the back. For roughing and smoothing (b), the whole back is relieved so the plane contacts the work only at the front and the blade. Both of these basic contours can be modified (c and d) to include more than one contact point in front of the blade. Exaggerated for illustration.

Left, after repeated sharpenings, the narrow flat at the edge of the hollow grind on the back of the blade is worn away, and the hollow grind must be tapped out to provide enough metal to produce another flat. Back the blade on the corner of a wooden or steel block and tap lightly and repeatedly with the corner of a small hammer in the center of the bevel. Be sure the blade is supported directly behind where the hammer strikes; vibration can easily crack the blade. Below, when enough of the hollow grind has been tapped out, the back must be flattened on a steel plate sprinkled with carborundum and water. Use a length of wood to back up the blade and to provide leverage for gradually increasing the pressure on the blade as you rub it vigorously back and forth. As the carborundum and water become a fine paste, your whole weight is brought to bear. The result is a narrow, mirror-smooth flat at the edge of the blade. You can then sharpen the bevel and the flat on stones.

blade. Then slowly increase the pressure. Keep the surface of the plate moist, and maintain even pressure on the blade with both hands. For leverage place a piece of wood about three times the length of the blade over it and grip the wood and the blade together. Use the wood as a handle and rub hard for a few minutes, then wipe the carborundum paste off the blade to examine the back. If it's even but dull and rough, and you have a flat at the middle of the edge about ¹⁄₁₆ in. wide, then gather the carborundum paste at the center of the plate and add a few more drops of water. This time press and rub as hard as you can until the paste is completely dry. Here's where working on the floor allows you to get your whole weight on top of the blade (photo, above). Look once again and if the back, all of it except for the hollow grind, is flat and shiny as a mirror, the work is done. If it is not, repeat the process. This is important because the more shine the edge has the sharper it will be. Western flat-back blades should be ground this way as well, so that the blade will keep its edge longer.

For a very narrow chisel (less than ¼ in.), it is not necessary to strike with a hammer. Use the carborundum powder and the steel plate. Obviously, the hollow grind will be shallower, but it will do the job.

Next, the corners of the blade are ground to an angle in order to prevent shavings from jamming in the plane body. Then the beveled edge is sharpened as described earlier. The

dimples left in the beveled surface from tapping out the hollow grind will disappear within two or three sharpenings.

Plane preparation—Sharpening is only part of the story; the plane body too must be prepared. "Japanese Planes" by Ted Chase (see pages 18 to 22) gives some good information. To it I should add that there are two basic contours for the sole of the Japanese plane—one for truing and one for roughing or smoothing. For truing, the sole is relieved so the plane contacts the work at the front, at the blade and at the back (figure 5a). This contour planes a perfectly flat surface because it removes only the high spots of the work, its depth of cut being limited both in front and in back of the blade.

For both roughing and smoothing planes, the whole sole behind the blade is relieved (figure 5b). Thus the plane contacts the work at only two points: at the front and at the blade. This configuration can take much larger shavings. In smoothing planes, the same contour allows the plane to follow the surface exactly, leaving a consistent shine to the wood. Both these configurations can be modified according to the requirements of the craftsman to include more than one contact point in front of the blade (figures 5c and 5d). □

Toshio Odate, of Woodbury, Conn., is a wood sculptor who teaches art at Pratt Institute in New York City. This article was prepared with the help of Audrey Grossman.

Sharpening to a Polished Edge
A cool, easy grind and a hard felt buff

by Charles F. Riordan

I've heard so many craftsmen complain about the length of time (and the expenditures for equipment) involved in bringing tools to a razor-sharp edge that I feel I must pass on the sharpening method I've evolved in the fifty-odd years I've been making shavings and sawdust.

My first mentor taught me to do it all by hand, using three grades of oilstones, with the final edge honed on a waterstone like those used to prepare a straight razor for the final stropping. After all these years I can still hear him saying, "If you can't shave with it, don't try to carve with it." While I can't disagree with his goal, his process was, at best, tedious. I began to search for methods that would let me spend more time using my tools than I was spending sharpening them.

An interest in gunsmithing led me to take courses in machine-shop practice, patternmaking and toolmaking. This, coupled with several years of machine-shop experience during World War II, taught me that there was a great deal more to sharpening a tool than scrubbing it back and forth on a flat stone, oil or otherwise.

I learned, to my surprise, that a coarse-grit grinding wheel properly dressed with a diamond dresser could remove metal faster than a fine-grit wheel, and leave a very good finish, with less chance of burning. And I found that using mist to cool the edge while grinding practically eliminates burning.

Riordan's full rig consists of an 8-in., 36-grit aluminum-oxide wheel, a misting device, a rest that maintains the proper angle, and a hard felt wheel. To sharpen plane irons, below, he uses a tool holder that slides parallel to the diamond-dressed face of the wheel. The safety shields have been lifted for the photos.

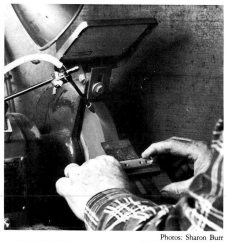

Riordan rotates a gouge, supported by an adjustable V-block, until the bevel is evenly ground. A misting nozzle directs its spray at the cutting edge. Mist, together with a light touch, keeps things so cool that there are hardly any sparks.

Photos: Sharon Burr

Then I discovered that buffing the ground edge on a hard felt wheel charged with gray compound would leave a razor edge. I also learned that to produce a good, even bevel on a tool, a positive rest (for gouges and small chisels) and a holding jig (for plane blades and wide chisels or skews) are absolute necessities. I have seen the results of freehand grinding by craftsmen who really thought that they were getting good results, until they tried sharpening with my rig.

The grinder I use is an old model Craftsman (Sears) ¾-HP with an 8-in., 36-grit wheel. The wheel is 1 in. wide and leaves a hollow grind that is neither too shallow nor too deep. You can adapt my system to whatever grinder you have. I removed the tool rest that came with the machine and fitted a 20-in. long arm that extends down in front of the grinding wheel. It is made from two pieces of 1-in. angle iron (preferably stainless steel) welded or bolted together by means of separators at each end so that there is a ⁵⁄₁₆-in. slot running its whole length. I bolted the arm to the clamp that came with the grinder, which allows the arm to pivot up and down. It can be clamped at whatever angle is necessary. As a socket for tool handles, I made a wooden V-block about 4 in. long and attached it to the arm by means of some strap iron and a carriage bolt extending through the slot. It can be secured at any point by tightening a wing nut. These two adjustments make it easy to get just the right bevel, whether the tool is a long-and-strong turning gouge or a small carving gouge.

For sharpening plane blades, skew chisels, skew turning tools and chisels that are wider than the wheel, I use a tool holder that rides on a 1-in. wide, 7-in. long piece of strap iron that can be adjusted parallel to the axis of the wheel. I wax the tool rest—it makes the jig slide much more easily. The strap iron can remain in place, as it will not get in the way when you are using the V-block.

I use the strap-iron rest in dressing the wheel with the diamond dresser—a small diamond chip mounted on the end of a handle. When the diamond contacts the spinning wheel, it removes glaze and trims off any high spots. You won't get a good edge unless your wheel is free of glaze, perfectly round and vibration-free. The ideal way to diamond-dress a wheel, of course, is to have the dresser mounted in a fixture that has a micrometer adjustment into the face of the wheel and a screw-feed across it. However, a little practice with the dresser, moving it slowly across the face of the wheel with very light, even pressure, can make you very adept at it. Diamond dressers can be obtained from any machine-tool dealer who handles grinding machines. A good one costs about $60, but it will last a long time—I've had mine for 25 years.

I use a compressed-air-driven misting device to cool the cutting edge while I grind. I won't go so far as to say that you can't burn an edge using mist, but it sure makes it a whale of a lot more difficult. The mist also keeps the wheel cleaner and thus minimizes dressing. I usually use plain water in the misting device, but coolant concentrates are available from mill suppliers and I would especially recommend the use of one with a good rust inhibitor if the water in your area tends to be acidic. The misting device I use is manufactured by Kool Mist Corp., 13141 Molette St., Santa Fe Springs, Calif. 90670; it costs about $22, and works fine at 40-lb. air pressure. If you do not have a compressor and do not wish to invest in one, you might try using plant sprayers or some other source of sprayed water instead. But mist, generated by high pressure, is a much more efficient coolant than water

After grinding, Riordan buffs a secondary bevel onto his tool edges, using a hard felt wheel charged with gray compound. He holds the tool so rotation is away from the edge, otherwise the wheel might catch the edge and hurl the tool.

droplets—people who use water come close to drowning.

Once I have ground the edge to the point where some people would accept it as sharp, I turn to the felt wheel, buffing the tool as shown in the photo above. This leaves a secondary bevel that has the strength to make many cuts before needing a touch-up. As shown in the drawing at left, a felt wheel as large as, or larger than, the grindstone can leave a fairly flat bevel (A), whereas the usual kind of polishing wheel, sewn-cloth, would undesirably round the edge (B). You can get a ⅝-in. wide, 8-in. hard felt wheel for about $50 from Paul H. Gesswein and Co., 255 Hancock Ave., Bridgeport, Conn. 06605.

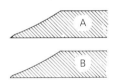

When I buff, I hold the heel of the bevel slightly away from the wheel, which results in a secondary bevel about ¹⁄₁₆ in. wide across the cutting edge. Use very little pressure—too much and the cutting edge will be burned, and you will have to start over. In fact, most of the time I shut off the motor and get a good edge as the motor runs down.

For touching up the tool while working, I make three or four passes over a smooth leather strop, leading with the heel of the bevel. The strop is simply a piece of leather belting stretched over a heavy hardwood block and soaked with a light mineral oil. I charge the strop by vigorously rubbing gray compound into it. One application lasts a long time. This strop restores the cutting edge amazingly well and cuts down on the number of trips to the buffing wheel.

No doubt, there will be those who will read this article and not be moved to try the method. For those who do decide to give it a whirl, however, I can guarantee that you will have no regrets—and very sharp tools, quickly and efficiently. □

Charles Riordan makes reproductions of period furniture and repairs antiques in Dansville, N.Y.

Index

FINE WOODWORKING
Editorial Staff, 1975-1984:

Paul Bertorelli
Mary Blaylock
Dick Burrows
Jim Cummins
Katie de Koster
Ruth Dobsevage
Tage Frid
Roger Holmes
John Kelsey
Linda Kirk
John Lively
Rick Mastelli
Ann E. Michael
Nina Perry
Jim Richey
Paul Roman
David Sloan
Nancy Stabile
Laura Tringali
Linda D. Whipkey

FINE WOODWORKING
Art Staff, 1975-1984

Roger Barnes
Deborah Fillion
Lee Hov
Betsy Levine
Lisa Long
E. Marino III
Karen Pease
Roland Wolf

FINE WOODWORKING
Production Staff, 1975-1984

Claudia Applegate
Barbara Bahr
Pat Byers
Deborah Cooper
Michelle Fryman
Mary Galpin
Barbara Hannah
Annette Hilty
Nancy Knapp
Johnette Luxeder
Gary Mancini
Laura Martin
Mary Eileen McCarthy
JoAnn Muir
Cynthia Nyitray
Kathryn Olsen

 **To subscribe**

If you enjoyed this book, you'll enjoy *Fine Woodworking* magazine.
Use this card to subscribe.

1 year (6 issues) for just $16—$5 off the newsstand price.
Canadian subscriptions: $19/year; other foreign: $20/year. (U.S. funds, please)

Name _____

Address _____

City _____ State _____ Zip _____

☐ My payment is enclosed. ☐ Please bill me.

☐ Please send me more information about Taunton Press Books.

☐ Please send me information about *Fine Woodworking* videotapes.

Fine WoodWorking **To subscribe**

If you enjoyed this book, you'll enjoy *Fine Woodworking* magazine.
Use this card to subscribe.

1 year (6 issues) for just $16—$5 off the newsstand price.
Canadian subscriptions: $19/year; other foreign: $20/year. (U.S. funds, please)

Name _____

Address _____

City _____ State _____ Zip _____

☐ My payment is enclosed. ☐ Please bill me.

☐ Please send me more information about Taunton Press Books.

☐ Please send me information about *Fine Woodworking* videotapes.

BUSINESS REPLY CARD
FIRST CLASS PERMIT No. 19 NEWTOWN, CT

POSTAGE WILL BE PAID BY ADDRESSEE

The Taunton Press
52 Church Hill Road
Box 355
Newtown, CT 06470

BUSINESS REPLY CARD
FIRST CLASS PERMIT No. 19 NEWTOWN, CT

POSTAGE WILL BE PAID BY ADDRESSEE

The Taunton Press
52 Church Hill Road
Box 355
Newtown, CT 06470